How to Cash In on Little-Known, Local Real Estate Investment Opportunities

How to Cash In on Little-Known, Local Real Estate Investment Opportunities

Samuel T. Barash

Prentice-Hall, Inc., Englewood Cliffs, N.J.

Prentice-Hall International, Inc., *London*
Prentice-Hall of Australia, Pty. Ltd., *Sydney*
Prentice-Hall of Canada, Ltd., *Toronto*
Prentice-Hall of India Private Ltd., *New Delhi*
Prentice-Hall of Japan, Inc., *Tokyo*
Prentice-Hall of Southeast Asia Pte. Ltd., *Singapore*
Whitehall Books, Ltd., *Wellington, New Zealand*

© 1980 by
Prentice-Hall, Inc.
Englewood Cliffs, N.J.

Library of Congress Cataloging in Publication Data

Barash, Samuel T
  How to cash in on little-known local real estate
investment opportunities.

  Includes index.
  1. Real estate investment. I. Title.
HD1375.B267   332.63′24   80-14895
ISBN 0-13-403188-1

Printed in the United States of America

ACKNOWLEDGMENT

With thanks to
Doug Strebel, Dr. Arthur Wisot, Arnold Resnick, Esq.
Jay Stahl III, Joseph Ruggiero, Frank Fini—
and with love and gratitude to
Julia Barash Esq. and Kit Barash.

Also by the author:
STANDARD REAL ESTATE APPRAISING MANUAL
HOW TO REDUCE YOUR REAL ESTATE TAXES

How This Book Will Help You Make More Money in Real Estate

In the stock market, trading in shares by "insiders" is carefully monitored and controlled by the Securities and Exchange Commission. Trades are reported and published so that corporate directors and others in the know can't take advantage of new developments within a company without the public's learning of their moves.

But in real estate investing, no such control exists. Too often the insiders, the pros, the people in the know, learn of investment opportunities that are beyond the scope of the general public's knowledge. They have deals all sewn up before knowledge of these opportunities leaks to the average investor.

This book will show you how you can find these deals *before* the insiders get to them. It will tell you precisely what these deals consist of, how you can find out about them, and how you can *act* on them so that you too can cash in on the many profitable but often hidden opportunities that exist in the real estate world.

Today, more than ever, our real estate world is full of unusual, little-known opportunities for making money. For example, here are just a few of the many practical and unique ideas you'll find in this book.

- Profits from small lakeside "gores" and rights-of-way.
- Profits from "Mini-Planned Unit Development" of small estates.
- Profits from annexing properties to suburban villages and cities.
- Profits from abandoned rights-of-way.

5

- Profits from quick "minor" land subdivisions.
- Profits from recreational land subdivision.
- Profits from highway interchange commercial plots.
- Profits from old gas station conversions.
- Profits from loft conversions.
- Profits from booming values in lots for fast-food outlets.
- Profits from mini-warehouses.
- Profits from tax sales and foreclosures.
- Profits from solar and insulation "rehabs."
- Profits and substantial *tax relief* from "historical properties."

Here are a few examples of actual small and large real estate investments that needed comparatively little money and yielded great returns.

ITEM: Four vacant acres were purchased for $25,000 per acre at an interstate highway interchange. Before closing on the original transaction, we subdivided and sold three commercial sites separately for a total of $210,000. Had simultaneous closings. Total cash investment—a $10,000 contract down payment. Total profit in 90 days—$110,000.

ITEM: We purchased a "mechanic's special" dilapidated rural area house with five hillside acres for $5,000. Sold it for $12,000 the following week. Closings held simultaneously. Total cash investment—$500. Total profit—$7000.

ITEM: An investor I know purchased a non-working 210-acre farm for $100,000 with $10,000 down. He sold the farmhouse with five acres for $15,000, a tenant house with five acres for $10,000, and timber rights for $75,000. He has now subdivided the remaining 200 acres into ten average 20-acre recreational land parcels on the existing paved road frontage, five of which are already sold, @ $30,000 each. Profit so far on the original $10,000 investment, before low real estate taxes and legal/ surveyor fees—$150,000. Eventual gross profit—$300,000.

ITEM: With two partners, purchased ten extremely steep lakeside acres for $20,000 with $5,000 down. Received local "minor" subdivision approval for four acre-each plots, using existing road frontage, and for one six-acre lakeside plot with serpentine easement access down the hillside bluff. Sold the four roadside plots for $9000 each and the lakeside parcel for $15,000. Total profit on the $5000 down payment investment plus $3,500 subdivision, legal and real estate tax costs equalled $27,500 net profit in nine months.

A key principle for real estate investing as developed in this book is this: *When you know what to look for, and how to evaluate it, you can go where no one else is going and get there before anyone else does.*

To do that, you have to have reliable sources of information. You'll find them here. You'll find out how to use government data banks for all the source data you need to make it big in real estate. You will see how and where to get valuable information free for big returns on residential investments. You'll find out how to get all the data required to locate and check out commercial and industrial investments. There is even a handy Source Data Checklist to help locate profitable real estate investments and prevent unanticipated losses.

You also have to know *value*. You'll find all the simplified appraisal procedures right here; for example, how to use the basic appraisal technique recognized in court and in the real estate marketplace . . . the *market approach* to value. Various modern day valuation concepts such as the "best comparable" technique are demonstrated in step-by-step procedures to help you buy and sell efficiently and profitably. You'll learn how to use the *income approach* on commercial properties and when to carefully use the *cost approach*, recognizing its limitations. You'll also find here not only how to value but also how to recognize *acceptable construction quality* in a lot, a house, an apartment building, a commercial structure, a factory or an industrial building complex. To value a property, you need to know how it is put together and you must also be able to recognize and avoid properties which are not feasible to build on or are not built properly. You'll find *all* the construction guides and checklists you need to arrive at reasonable value and acceptability conclusions.

In order to make money in unusual local real estate deals, it is important to act quickly and expertly yet be thoroughly familiar with the property and its area. In practically all cases, to do this safely and profitably, you have to invest *locally*. You'll find here complete information on why and how you are the one in the best position to know your own area and the people who live and work there. This book shows you how to build on your local knowledge and contacts. It also shows you how to convert what you already know about your area into big real estate profits as the pros do everyday. It gives you all the techniques of locating all these "hidden real estate gold mines," as well as all the methods for following up with proper, expert "checkout" procedures to safely ensure big real estate profits.

This book also shows why you don't have to have a great deal of capital to get rich in real estate. Money sometimes helps expedite deals, but uniformed investment often quickly loses this "up-front" money instead of making more. In addition to the normal high-interest bank and mortgage company loans, you'll find many little-known, often more reasonable financing techniques here. For example, there is the "purchase-money" mortgage from the seller . . . the "assumption" mortgage . . . the "contract-sale" financing method . . . the "second" and "third" mortgage without personal liability . . . and the local real estate "syndication" technique.

What *does* help is knowing what's going on in your area, knowing how to spot developing trends and changes and being "in" on the contemporary scene. The homes we inhabit, where we work and how we get to work have all dramatically changed in the past few decades. Our life style, the very size and structure of the American family have been altered in basic ways. Families are smaller. Most women now work. There are increasing numbers of divorced and single people.

So this book deals with the relevant contemporary scene in terms of the many special, local, unusual, little-known, often unorthodox and innovative methods and opportunities you can use to increase your profits in real estate.

In sum, you have everything you need here, all the inside ways and sources to use the knowledge provided and a wide range of tips that will help you get to these "hidden" deals first . . . all the ways to exploit these deals profitably . . . and all the financing methods to make these deals work with little or no cash of your own.

Samuel T. Barash

Table of Contents

1

Why the Best
Real Estate Investments
Are Virtually Unknown

Sandra H. grew up in her small northeastern hill town about 1000 feet down the road from a vacant, wooded, 4½-acre piece of land. When the estate owner put the parcel up for sale, Sandra purchased it and subdivided the parcel into four minimum one-acre building lots. After only nine months, she earned a net profit of $42,000—*more than four times her cash investment!* Aware of a local scarcity of approved building lots, Sandra had used her local knowledge and contacts and applied the little-known technique called minor subdivision, spelled out later in this book, to achieve this magnificent profit so quickly. You can do it too.

Modern America is creating many such little-known, new, challenging real estate profit opportunities. This first chapter tells what's fueling this modern real estate boom and what makes real estate investments little known.

It goes on to define the exact specifications of unorthodox real estate opportunities. There is also a revealing section on how the top-flight professionals keep their best real estate deals for themselves. There is a variety of examples of extremely successful pro- and non-pro investors who have penetrated these hidden real estate deal "secrets" . . . which illustrate how anyone wanting high profits can get in on this action in little-known, unorthodox real estate profit opportunities.

HOW TO PROFIT FROM OUR MODERN REAL ESTATE BOOM

To crystal-ball and profit from our real estate future, you have to keep up with what's going on with our land and its people. The young people of today who are mainly changing our real estate future are part of the post-WWII "baby boom," which crested in 1957. They are remaking America with their wants and goals. In the eighties, they'll number over 30 million. They're home oriented. They are flocking to our rural towns. They are "urban-pioneering" our inner cities. They've lowered the birth rate. They're marrying later. They've made us into a double-income family market. They've made single-person households usual. They have changed our society and the real estate marketplace. They've brushed aside high, constantly inflating real estate costs and are buying properties feverishly to protect their future against this same inflation. They are the real estate market of the future.

Real estate in America is alive and well. The future looks bright and profitable, particularly for alert, local investors in our expanding small towns and rural areas and in our revitalizing city neighborhoods.

Here are six investors I know who profited from such modern little-known real estate investment opportunities:

Examples of Real Estate Investors Who Made Big Profits

• Dr. Lawrence G. bought a 50-acre abandoned dairy farm and sold it a year later for about three times what he had paid. A horse enthusiast, he resold the farm and buildings for horse farm use to people he met through his hobby. This investor bought, sold and made big profits in this little-known agricultural usage because he knew that the farmland was not rocky, that it rolled gently, and that its spring water was high in calcium—all good specifications for raising horses.

• Stanley H., a former bank teller, found out how to make big money from banks . . . in real estate. When his midwestern state (along with other states like New York and California) recently authorized lending institutions to open branch banks, he profited from this legislation. With two partner-investors, he bought a small, vacant, 2½-acre commercial site on a main road on the outskirts of his small town near a large existing development of about 300 homes. They applied for and received approval for a small neighborhood shopping center of 10,000 square feet for ten attached convenience type stores plus one free-standing 2500 sq. ft. building. They rented the free-standing building to a bank on a long-term lease for more than enough to finance construction of their whole project. Like fast-food and convenience stores, convenience branch banks are proliferating throughout our land wherever state laws permit—and are paying top real estate dollars to alert landowners and builders. Stanley H., the former bank teller, is still involved with banks; he now holds leases on five bank buildings in his region.

• Mary and John R. worked diligently for 20 years in their small hometown cleaning store. They earned a living. Recently they also started to work diligently during their spare time at buying a 25-acre land tract on their town line and getting it annexed to the village so it could benefit from village water and sewer lines. When they received town and village approval for the annexation, they sold the land to a developer. This part-time diligence in this little-known real estate field paid off royally: $150,000 profit for two years' work.

• Two real estate salespersons I know like to read about zoning ordinances and changes. In their local newspaper's legal notices, they noticed one day that a change was proposed from residential to commercial zoning for one area of their village. For $1000, they took a 90-day option on a 150' × 200' well-located, level corner plot on a street with a heavy traffic count in the proposed commercial zone. After enactment of the ordinance, they sold their option for $14,000.

• Jack M., a former A&P assistant store manager, is a full-time real estate investor now. He buys and sells one-family houses only. His method of operation is little known yet simple. He follows up every sale of a house in his area by checking assessors' records so he is aware of current values at all times. When he sees a house just advertised for sale and priced under market, he buys it. Or if he notes that a house has been for sale overlong, say more than six months, he makes a low offer well below market value, which is often accepted by a seller under pressure. He fixes and paints up when necessary but most of the time he is able to resell as is for profit. He also rents some of the houses he buys while he waits for house prices to rise even further. Jack has invested some of his profits from home sales into commerical investments—including purchases of the A&P store lease where he had worked previously.

All these investors had one successful trait in common. Each cashed in local knowledge and contacts for big profits from varied little-known real estate investments. You can do it too.

WHAT MAKES A REAL ESTATE INVESTMENT
LITTLE KNOWN?

If you want to make big money in real estate you must first be attuned to its workings. Real estate is a marketplace where money and other valuable considerations like mortgages are exchanged for vacant land and improved (built-upon) properties.

Like the stock market, the real estate market fluctuates up and down, depending on many interacting factors including supply, demand, location. Unlike the stock market or other regulated markets which are generally housed and controlled in central locations, real estate "trading" or investment takes place constantly, everywhere. Yet the market is ever present in every deal everywhere.

The ancient economic laws of supply and demand apply in all real estate deals. The one who can buy low and sell high makes the investment killing. He is also the one who can identify the "turnaround situation," the property which many would want but don't yet know about, the "little-known" real estate profit opportunity.

What makes a real estate investment "little known"? This is a relative term. For instance, if a real estate investment is known only to the one who presently owns it and to only a few others who may not want to or may not know how to buy it for profit, then it is little known.

The above examples are but the start of the following checklist. All the checklist items are not the end-all of little-known real estate opportunities, but they do help to show the way to what is little known and profit making. The successful technique is to get there first, analyze and recognize the opportunity and then develop the property's profit-making potential with knowledge and imagination for resale and/or income. Use this checklist to help locate profitable investments. Also, apply it as a yardstick to measure possible real estate investments for profit potential.

CHECKLIST FOR LITTLE-KNOWN REAL ESTATE INVESTMENTS

- Is this a potential turnaround real estate situation?
- Is the property new on the market? Not yet generally known?
- If the property has been overlong on the market, has it been just reduced in price by a financially pressed seller to below market value?
- Regardless of how long it has been for sale, is it offered at less than market value?
- Does it have unique value like lake, view or other popular attraction?
- Could it benefit from popular interest in modern concepts such as solar and insulation rehabilitation?
- Is it a potential moneymaker because of pending locality changes like road widenings or proposed road interchanges?

- Is its neighborhood beginning to undergo use changes like loft conversions to artists' studios or to condominium apartments? Is the adjacent neighborhood thus changing, showing signs of spillover?
- Is there a zoning change pending which will make low-return properties potential commercial or other denser use money-makers?
- Is there a needed little-known money-making use like miniwarehouses for a piece of low-priced industrial land in the area you know?
- Is there land for sale where you hunt, fish or camp? The hidden trails you tread could lead to where you can reap tomorrow's resale or subdivision profits.
- Are the railroad ties you skipped along in your youth now abandoned? Is the railroad right-of-way for sale? Any other long narrow right-of-way "gore" type of land for sale in your area? These can often be bought up on a wholesale basis and resold on a retail subdivision basis to adjacent property owners for big profits.
- Did George Washington sleep somewhere near you? Are government regulations, little read by most, opening up tremendous profit and tax write-off investment opportunities like historical properties in your area?
- Can you annex a property you own or buy, to the adjacent community which has public utilities like sewer and water? Spectacular increases in value and profits result from such annexation.

HOW PROS KEEP THE BEST DEALS TO THEMSELVES

Be he real estate broker, attorney-investor, mortgage banker or professional real estate investor, the professional who deals daily in real estate usually keeps the best deals for himself. My purpose here is not to criticize such profit-making, very human traits. It is only to describe to you how they do it so their professional techniques can be used successfully and their hidden real estate gold mines unearthed.

The key ways pros use to locate and keep the best details to themselves are as follows:

- They get there first.
- They go where no one else is going.
- They know their local area of investment thoroughly. They always keep up with developing trends in their area.
- They develop sources of information on properties for sale or properties which can be developed for profit.
- They know how to appraise for current value, for potential profit from development, for highest and best use.

- They use this valuation knowledge to make their extremely profitable decisions on when to buy, develop, operate, lease and sell.
- They know how to finance their deals using little or none of their own money.
- They know which location makes vacant land valuable.
- They recognize when a building is suitable for its use, whether it is well constructed, and what can be done to enhance its value.
- They can identify a deal's prospects for high, fast or assured continuing returns.
- They move into deals quickly, generally *before* the investment opportunity becomes known to the public.

HOW YOU CAN GET IN ON
THESE LITTLE-KNOWN, HIGH-PROFIT DEALS

You don't have to be the favorite son of a successful investor pro to get in on this action in these hidden, little-known investment opportunities. You can be part of the industry—a broker, salesman, attorney, accountant or contractor involved in real estate. These premises, techniques and directions for finding and profiting from these little-known deals will show you the way to profit enormously from your daily work. Or you can be just anyone—anyone who wants to make high profits from small investments. And real estate, particularly in these little-known, unorthodox real estate investments, is where this action in high returns is found.

Three Keys to Successful Real Estate Investing

For starters, there are three basic premises in real estate investing:

1. It is still the one investment field where very large assets can be handled with very little cash.
2. It is still the one investment field where population movement and increase create rising demand with a static supply practically guaranteeing increased value.
3. It is still the one investment field which can effectively shelter income from taxes.

The successful investor is the one who starts with these premises and uses the techniques described here to profit from his real estate investments. Many of these techniques can be observed in the following actual real estate investments.

How One Investor Put His Children Through College

While camping out near Colorado Springs, Colorado in the early seventies, a good friend of mine, a person who had never before speculated in real estate, looked to the west, bemused by the magnificent view of Pikes Peak. Entranced by the view, he mused also on his four children, who would soon be of college age, and on their coming need for tuition. This view of Pikes Peak resulted within two days in his leaving a deposit on 40 acres of rolling land with a local broker. The land had frontage on two roads. It was good land, but the whole area was populated at the time by my one friend and his vision. He paid $300 an acre, with a $2500 down payment and the balance on a long purchase-money mortgage taken by the seller. Taxes were a minuscule $12 a year.

Now his taxes have gone up to $350 a year. But so has the population in the area. My friend recently subdivided the land into six five-acre lots and one ten-acre "flag" lot. Three of his children are in college now, *at the same time*, with one soon to enter. He has sold off three of the five-acre lots @ $1550 per acre each. He plans to sell one more @ $1800 an acre next year (when his fourth child enters college).

In addition to showing how to put one's children through college by using a unique real estate investment, this example demonstrates a number of our key investment techniques. (Also, see Chapter 8 for details on how to subdivide such a minor subdivision and for a definition of what a "flag" lot is.)

- This investment case shows imagination and innovation in investment. Any deal needs an amenity quality, a lake, a view, a golf course, a great traffic count for commercial investment. This one had Pikes Peak.
- My friend was here *first*.
- Little cash was required; big profits returned. The seller financed the deal by taking back a large purchase-money mortgage. (This is where the seller takes a certain amount of cash from the buyer and holds a mortgage for the balance, using the property as security.)
- My friend bought in the path of development. Colorado Springs, with its Air Force Academy and with other growth factors, was only six miles away and expanding in this direction along good arterial roads.
- He is cashing in on his little-known local investment. Original cost—$12,000. Engineering and subdivision costs—$2500. Total costs—$14,500, plus very moderate (tax-deductible) interest and real estate taxes. Total actual and anticipated income from lot sales in a very active market—$72,500.

How a "Fix-Up" Investor Doubled Her Money in Three Months

Anne R., formerly a housewife, recently became a part-time real estate saleswoman in a rural-suburban southeastern New York area. Real estate commissions were comparatively good but, as usual in real estate brokerage, her deals took time to close.

While she worked and waited for her commissions, Anne continued to talk to people—about real estate. One of the people she talked to was a mortgage banker who happened to mention an impending foreclosure. Anne and her husband spoke to the property owners who were in the process of separation. They bought from the parting couple their 960-square-foot one-story dwelling (just prior to foreclosure) on a rustic, wooded acre on a town road. It had an attached 12' × 24' garage which had been mainly converted into two small bedrooms and storage area. The selling price was $25,000.

Down the same rural road where this house was located, only a mile away, was her "best comparable"—a 960-square-foot one-story house on one acre. This good comparable had really only two differences—a built-in garage instead of a converted garage and better exterior aluminum instead of asbestos siding. These differences were easily adjusted for value by standard market appraisal comparison methods. The comparable house just down the road had sold for $48,500 six months earlier in an arm's length transaction with neither buyer nor seller acting under duress.

In three months, Anne and her husband personally painted the exterior, carpeted the interior, and sold it for $48,000. This all took place in a part of the Northeast where real estate values were comparatively static—except for people like Anne and her husband. This example shows the following:

   • From local knowledge and sources, the investor located an investment opportunity.
   • Anne R. used good appraisal techniques to determine that the house was a good buy well below market at $25,000. She also determined what it should sell for when "fixed up."
   • With their "sweat equity," the buyers of the subject dwelling fixed up the dwelling so that it could sell for this maximum profit. Priced right and looking just right for showing, the house sold quickly.
   • Anne R. arranged for FHA financing for the buyer, who bought the spruced-up house for $48,000. This was in New York State at a time when no conventional mortgages were being committed by banks. So, in a static real estate market, in a state where mortgages were very hard to get, this imaginative, hard-working couple bought, financed with an

FHA mortgage and sold this home. They made a net profit of over $20,000 in less than 90 days.

This beginning chapter has defined little-known and unorthodox real estate investments. Succeeding chapters will show how to uncover these hidden, high-profit, quick-return deals . . . how to build on your local knowledge and contacts . . . how to apply the step-by-step procedures you'll find here to locate and profit from these investment opportunities.

2

How Pros Uncover the Best Deals—and How You Can Do the Same Thing

To make big money in real estate, you not only have to be able to identify little-known unorthodox investments, you also have to know where and how to find them before others bid them up. This chapter gives detailed instructions on how real estate professionals do this and how you can do it too. It shows what this dynamic, ever-changing real estate investment business is all about. It zeros in on the big *local* real estate profits all around you. It also gives specific directions on how to spot growth patterns. You'll see that you don't have to just wait for things to happen . . . you're shown here how to make them happen with investment techniques like zoning changes. This chapter also gives you a very important summary list of all the keys to success and the common denominators for real estate profits.

THE CONTINUING EFFECT OF THE BABY BOOM

Modern America has been in a state of constant growth and change during the past three decades. Major social, population and technological factors like autos and interstate highways have combined to change our formerly urban-rural country to its present suburban-urban state. The process is still dynamic. For example, the vast baby boom of 1947 to 1957 is a key economic force in housing and in the commercial and industrial services which support expansion of suburban and urban dwellings. This mammoth generation of American men and women passing through infancy, youth, middle age and old age is like a bulge passing through an overfed boa constrictor. Being aware of this phenomenon is most important for proper understanding of real estate change and for successful investment. A big proportion of this bulge is now of the family-forming, home-buying age. Even though many of these modern "households" are single and childless, they still buy houses and condominiums and they support commercial and industrial service businesses in their area, the same as their family-type forebears did. This "bulge" is causing increases in real estate values and profits, expansion of rural small town areas and revitalization of our cities.

Many new, little-known real estate investment opportunities are being created by these technological and social changes. The neighborhood gas stations bypassed by newer roads and made obsolete by high-volume gas company stations can become neighborhood "convenience" stores. The declining blocks of urban row houses become the turnaround "historical" rehabilitated townhouses because of tax legislation favoring historical preservation. The thousands of new suburban neighborhoods with smaller dwellings and apartments needing additional storage space create new investment opportunities like mini-warehouses. All this and much more is new and just becoming known to the professional investor as our society and its major asset, real estate, continue to change in response to all these factors.

HOW TO SPOT BIG LOCAL REAL ESTATE
PROFITS ALL AROUND YOU

This changed and changing contemporary scene is the setting for those who want to make money in real estate. This is true whether you live and work in one of the tens of thousands of new small towns or in a city. You don't have to put your money into high-pressure out-of-state land investments which others can lose for you. All you have to do is look around where you live or work or play.

Local real estate investment is the name of the game. Reduced to the simplest investment terms, every home and property owner is a local investor whose home or property is not only his investment but also his hedge against inflation. Long distance ownership of real estate can be profitable but also can lead to losses. When you invest locally, you can keep an eye on your property. If it needs management, you're there. If an opportunity for profit arises, you're around to grasp it. There are "miracle miles" transforming town roads to commercial investment bonanzas in every expanding exurban area. And there are tens of thousands of urban neighborhoods being revitalized block by block, brownstone by brownstone, in all our cities. Your family, social, business and fraternal contacts also could be your path to real estate investment riches.

How Two Local Investors Made Big Profits

A plumber whom I know, "Big John," can usually be found in his coveralls at 8:00 A.M. having coffee in the local diner. In the 15 years I have known him, he has quietly bought up prime commercial, residential and industrial land and buildings through his working knowledge of the town, its people and its growth. Big John is a millionaire many times over. However, I still see him each morning at 8:00 A.M. in his coveralls having coffee in the diner. But now he also owns the diner!

Or take Mike N., partner in a local bowling alley. When he needed more parking space for his patrons, a hill of shale had to be flattened at the rear of the bowling alley. Excavation and dump truck removal were at very high cubic-yard cost. So instead, Mike looked down the road and bought a real estate "hole" nobody wanted. This hole was right next to the main road entering the community. Mike also bought a bulldozer and dump trucks, hired an operator by the hour to level the hill at the bowling alley by excavating and dumping it into the hole down the road. Now the bowling alley patrons have enough parking space, the hole is a prime piece of *level* commercial real estate—and Mike has a long net, net land lease with a Pizza-Hut fast food store which has been built on the filled hole. All this imaginative investing was done *locally*.

Mike and John are but two examples I know of alert investors who have made fortunes locally in real estate. A later section in this chapter will list all these local and other keys to success for real estate profits. Succeeding chapters will develop this idea by showing you all the local sources you can exploit for investments as well as all the details and techniques for developing specific local real estate profit opportunities.

HOW TO SPOT LOCAL GROWTH PATTERNS

To make real estate profits, you have to be where the action is. Better still, you can be first to make the big profits if you know and invest where the action will be. To do this, you can always depend on one thing in real estate—real estate activity never stands still. Because it is solid, it is there, it is finite, investors have always dealt in real estate, particularly during inflation-ridden times like ours. Take land, for instance; it is finite because it does not regenerate or make more land. Even though he can't create more, the real estate investor can subdivide land and make small pieces out of big pieces. He can build higher, deeper, denser. To know when to make your move, you must not only know your local region; you must also follow its patterns of activity, its growth, its decline, its turnaround areas. The following data sources must all be used if you are to come home a real estate profit winner.

• *A town or city block or city neighborhood* is like a living organism. Although composed of bricks, stone, wood and mortar, each community houses its inhabitants whose daily work and aspirations give life to their community. They also make up the real estate market. So watch the demographic trends; check how and where the population waxes and wanes. Know the neighborhoods, walk the blocks, keep up with what's going on.

• *Department of Census.* This is the one best source for vital population statistics and for other useful studies like household and family formation characteristics. This is where you get the trends on where the people are moving into and out of your area and region. This is where you spot overall growth patterns.

• *County Planning Offices.* These offices have important growth statistics, specific area studies, helpful maps and professional planners. Real estate investing means you're betting on future events. County planning offices are where you can hedge your bets with the best professional data on local growth patterns. For a few dollars you can get their planning data books which give invaluable information (and local maps) on local land use, topographic features, labor supply, industry employment, lending institutions, income levels in area, community facilities, population housing, transportation utilities and directories of local approval boards and officers.

• *Local Planning Boards.* This is where all local property owners must get approvals to change or improve their property. This is where you find out where the action is in the community.

• *Building Inspector.* This is the best place to spot actual growth by reviewing what type, where and how many building permits were issued. For example, if you want to know where new house or condominium building developments will be located in your community, you find out from the planning board and building inspector offices. You find out there which developments are being considered and which have been approved. I have often been able to buy or option adjacent residential or commercial land for future profits as soon as these developments were started.

The following is an illustrative case history of an investor who touched all these information bases and ensured his big profits.

An Investor Who Profited from Local Changes

I recently completed a land appraisal for Henry S., a real estate investor. He had moved into his small suburban town only about three years ago and immediately devoted much of his time to familiarizing himself completely with what was going on in his area. He liked to jog so he knew every block, every vacant parcel. He read all the local newspapers carefully, including the real estate and legal notices. He spent time in the offices of the municipal building planner and the assessor, learning what was happening. He found out that public sewers would be installed in one area within two years. He also learned that local condominium enabling laws had recently been enacted.

So two years ago, Henry S. bought a ten-acre wooded parcel for $5,000 an acre on the town highway where the express bus to the city runs. This parcel was in the path of the proposed sewers and zoned for up to 80 apartment or condominium units (with public sewers).

I recently appraised his land for $2,500 a unit or $20,000 an acre. He sold the land, subject to final condominum approval, to a developer for $215,000. Approval was later granted and the deal consummated. Gross profit return for Henry's jogging and local studies—$165,000!

GUIDELINES ON MAKING PROFITS THROUGH ZONING CHANGES

Real estate pros don't wait for the lightning of real estate profits to strike. They often help to make profits happen. One of the most frequent ways they do this is with zoning changes. It is true that some very rural areas of our country still don't have zoning laws, maps or other planning controls. Most of the areas we live and work in however do control land use by limiting where and what kind of residential or commercial or industrial property can be built or altered. This zoning or restricting of uses by type and location is probably the single most important factor that makes value in real estate. Many have argued that the history of zoning proves that we would have been just as well or better off without it, as some areas, even cities without zoning, have shown.

However, for better or worse, zoning is almost everywhere. It can also make or break real estate investors. The following step-by-step procedure should always be followed to insure that you don't buy a property with an illegal use and that you always take proper precautions to protect your investment when it is zoned or when future value is dependent on a zoning change. However, the chance for spectacular profits is really there with zoning changes, such as changing from residential to commercial or one-family detached residential to multi-family or attached townhouses. It pays very well to know how to go about it. It pays even better to succeed. With diminishing land availability and increasing population pressures, the economic need for such denser zoning is there. If you get these zoning changes, profits are assured because the property has become more valuable.

If more units can be built per acre, the property is worth more. For example, if zoning permits three houses an acre the land may be worth, say $4,000 per unit or $12,000 an acre to a builder developer. If however, eight condominium units can be built per acre, the same land would be valued at say $3,000 per unit or $24,000 per acre! This same principle also applies to other uses permitted by zoning. The same land once zoned for residential use can be worth ten times more if it is rezoned for commerical use.

A STEP-BY-STEP PROCEDURE
FOR REZONING APPLICATIONS

This is how you go about applying and getting zoning changes:

Step 1. Check zoning. Before buying any property, review the latest zoning map and ordinance. Is the present use legal? If vacant land, is it zoned for the use you propose? If it has a non-conforming use like commercial when it is zoned for residential, can the non-conforming use continue? For example, if the non-conforming use has been vacated for over a year, must the use be discontinued?

Step 2. Analyze the property. If the property you own or want to buy is so situated that it is logical for it to be changed in zoning, then continue to Step 3.

Step 3. If you are buying, buy the property on option, subject to getting your application for zoning change approved. Have the present owner agree in your contract that he will assist in your zoning applications.

Step 4. Prepare the zoning appeal. Zoning ordinances spell out how to file for zoning change or variance and what forms and/or maps have to be submitted. Visit the town clerk and the planning board clerk for this data. Owners of properties in the vicinity of the property under appeal have to be notified. It is often best to visit them personally and discuss what you plan to do, particularly if you are their neighbor-owner. If the property is large and the stakes high, it would be best to retain a lawyer experienced in such zoning matters.

THE KEYS TO SUCCESS AND THE COMMON DENOMINATORS FOR PROFITS

Developed throughout this book are many key principles for successful real estate investing, detailing how to spot and profit from little-known, local real estate investments. However, so that you can have a good overview, the following checklist summarizes these key successful real estate principles. It also lists for you in one place all the common denominators for high real estate profits. They are key principles which are based on my own 25 years of investment experience and on the experience of other successful investors I've appraised for and observed. They apply to residential, commercial and industrial investments, particularly to little-known, unorthodox, highly profitable deals:

CHECKLIST OF KEY ITEMS FOR REAL ESTATE PROFITS

1. Don't waste your time looking for "bargains." Often the "bargain" you check out turns out to be far above market by appraisal and construction check.
2. Do make certain you buy at market or below by doing a good valuation analysis.
3. Don't wait for the last profit buck.
4. Do your homework on growth patterns. Buy in the path of development.
5. Hire attorneys experienced in real estate law. Make sure they advise you legally; don't let them make your business decisions on the real estate.
6. The same goes for accountants, engineers and surveyors.
7. Be patient, detailed and fair in negotiation. Remember, most real estate deals don't close unless they're good for both sides.
8. Syndication of real estate deals to get additional buying power is fine as long as you stick with small local groups you personally know which invest in local areas you know. Stay away from large real estate investment syndicates. Your profits are generally absorbed by their fees. Sometimes your investment is too.
9. Location is first, last and always the most important key principle for real estate profits.
10. Check out the deal carefully. Do the market and other necessary studies. Appraise it objectively. If you're too hot for it, hire an independent appraiser to give you a report. It might cool you off.

11. If it's a building, check the construction. If there is any question, or if you believe you're not qualified, hire an engineer or construction inspector to give you a report. The report might turn out to be a better investment than the investment.

12. Stay away from absentee investments in real estate. The best way to lose money is to invest in out-of-state land "buys" from high pressure land promotors. The best way to make money is to get involved in land or buildings locally, in deals you can see, walk on, and keep up with on a local basis.

13. Hire good tax lawyers and accountants. One of the few excellent remaining tax shelters is real estate. You want to make sure that you pay your fair legal share, but no more, of your real estate profits. You want to be sure that you buy and sell in this fascinating real estate market with full regard for your total other income and how it is "sheltered."

14. Buy and sell with knowledge of any local and state tax exemptions which may apply.

15. Buy and sell with proper financing so that you use little or none of your own money and still avoid personal liability. Let the property always be the security for the mortgage.

16. Go where others are not going for unusual properties.

17. Get there first.

18. Don't buy environmentally unsound properties where modern controls will stop you from developing for profit.

19. Always buy on option when you plan to develop, build or get zoning changes on a property. The best laid plans of mice and real estate investors gang oft agley when planning boards reject applications.

20. Always buy location. The best property improvement can be the worst if in the wrong place.

21. Invest locally but don't be provincial. Innovations like mini-warehouses which begin in other regions like the Southwest are being introduced into the Northeast by imaginative local real estate investors.

22. Be alert to and buy in turnaround areas. Houses I appraised for $12,000 ten years ago in brownstone areas of Brooklyn, are going for $80,000 for shells, up to $200,000 for restored properties.

23. Buy in central areas of communities or where sewer and water lines are being extended if you are buying land for development. Property may be cheaper if you leapfrog out to the country. However, public utilities may never reach you. Private wells may not yield adequate water. Soil may not percolate for septic tanks. For cleaner water, a vast federal subsidy program is now helping to build local sewer and water plants throughout America. Keep up with what is planned in your area—and profit from it.

3

How Local Information and Other Data Sources Can Make Profits for You

This chapter defines exactly what "local" real estate investing means. It stresses the rewards of local investing contrasted to the possible perils of owning distant real estate. It specifies why local investment is so important in our changing real estate scene. You'll find out here where to go and how to use government data banks for the basic source data you need, often free for the asking. A companion source section includes a comprehensive Data Resources Guide checklist and gives you in one place the whole host of local officials and other people who can help you locate and profit from high-return local real estate deals. There is a straightforward six-part plan on how you can trade in your local knowledge and contacts for high real estate profits. There is also a section on how to pool limited real estate investment funds with other local people whenever you want to get into bigger profit opportunities. The last section includes a 50-state address list of state property tax offices and details the "secret world" of tax breaks on forest land, agricultural land, and other tax exemptions for those in the know.

DETERMINING YOUR OWN LOCAL REAL ESTATE INVESTMENT BOUNDARIES

To make money in little-known, unusual, local real estate deals you must first know your area well enough to immediately recognize a good deal. What does "local" mean? Are you limited to your block, your neighborhood, your country? Is there a geographical local limit? A mile? Ten miles? As far as the eye can see?

The answers to these questions of definition are in your own life style. They can also be answered with other questions. Are you a homeowner, renter, commuter, merchant, hunter, hiker, regular traveler, real estate broker, salesman, contractor or a 9-to-5 salaried person who likes to get away on weekends?

"Local" is defined differently and yet the same for all of us, depending on where and how we live, work and relax. The merchant who closes up shop on holidays to fish is investing locally when he buys up low-cost lands for subdivision 150 miles from home near his favorite trout stream. The apartment renter in the suburbs, always short of storage space, who invests with other local people to build a small mini-warehouse two miles from his apartment and from the thousands of other potential apartment-dweller warehouse space renters . . . the weekend or regular holiday traveler to favorite tourist spots who winds up franchising a budget motel or motels there . . . the real estate broker-salesman who spots and buys a "mechanic's special" house in his selling area suitable for "buy-up-fix-up" profits . . . the housewife turned real estate investor in a historical property on her block . . . the traveling salesman who regularly sells in his 1,000-mile familiar region and who spots and invests in a good commercial "hot corner" land deal many miles from home . . . the tenant in a multi-family apartment building who buys the building he's been living in . . . the doctor who puts his surplus funds into a professional building where he practices . . . all these and more local investors have one key real estate investing principle in common. Each invested in a real estate deal which he unearthed and could watch from *local* knowledge and contacts. Regardless of how close or far away in miles, each investor knew the property, its environs and its economic background intimately. Each was able to act upon this local knowledge by getting to these special little-known deals before others did.

In sum, a local real estate investment is whatever deal you invest in, whether it is where you live, work or play, no matter how far—as long as it's one located within the regular familiar bounds of your way of life.

THE PERILS OF ABSENTEE OWNERSHIP: WHY LOCAL INVESTMENT IS SO IMPORTANT

The perils of absentee real estate ownership are not just limited to boiler-room sales of land development lots located in deserts or swamps, far from investors. Any time you put your money into land or buildings in an area you do not live in or visit regularly, you are an absentee owner or landlord. Often you are fair game for the local property manager, general partner in your real estate limited partnership deal or other person who is supposed to watch out for your interests. This applies even to vacant land which can't be stolen, burned, mismanaged or deteriorated. You are not there to see if the land goes up for tax sale because of a bookkeeping error or nonpayment of taxes by the manager. You can't protect your interest and speak out or take action against a pending locally known zoning change which could reduce the land value dramatically. You're not around regularly to note and take advantage of changing road patterns which change land value, of economic conditions which would skyrocket or wipe out the land value overnight.

Real estate investment is the main vehicle for sheltering income from taxes and for keeping ahead of inflation. The perils of absentee ownership investing, the risks in putting your money in large syndicated investments and limited partnership all point the way towards do-it-yourself local real estate investing. Depending on the type of investment, there are degrees of risk. You can minimize these risks and maximize profits by starting from your local plateau of knowledge, experience and people you know. Local investment based on your own complete investigation can, of course, be professionally assisted by your hiring of local surveyors, local appraisers, attorneys and local professional managers and accountants as needed during ownership.

HOW YOU CAN TAP GOVERNMENT DATA BANKS TO MAKE IT BIG IN REAL ESTATE

Systematic accumulation of data in the real estate marketplace and from other sources is critical to successful real estate investment. Our government has become a major information supplier. The vast resources of our federal bureaucracy are available to you at practically no cost. It is an information treasure trove for investors. There are many agencies which have thousands of experts. Detailed, professional written data can be had for the asking. The following list is specific to those branches of our government which can assist real estate investors.

• *U.S. Superintendent of Documents, Washington, D.C.* The Superintendent will send you, on request, regular mailings which list *all* recent publications by U.S. Agencies. You can then order them at little or no cost. This mailing list will keep you alert to all current government data on real estate.

• *Department of Census.* This is the single most important source for population, household, family formation and other demographic data vital to informed real estate investing.

• *Housing and Urban Development* (HUD). This is the most important housing and development department which issues national building codes, housing data and other studies, and through its FHA has foreclosed houses for sale. It administers the National Flood Insurance program which has had recent major impact on land usage and development. Its booklet, "Questions and Answers—National Flood Insurance Program," is must reading for real estate investors.

• *Farmers Home Administration* (FmHA), Department of Agriculture. The FmHA makes rural home and farm loans and is a very important real estate financing agency for the general public in exurban areas. It also is an important source for data on home and farm sales and for other rural real estate data.

• *Department of Army Engineer Corps.* The Corps is the major source in its Directorate of Real Estate office for real estate data on its major condemnation and construction dams, river and flood control projects which affect the economy and real estate activity throughout all regions.

• *Small Business Administration.* The SBA is a major source for data on business trends, and does sell foreclosed parcels.

• *General Services Administration.* The GSA acquires, manages, services and sells to the public surplus government real property.

HOW LOCAL PEOPLE CAN HELP LOCATE
HIGH RETURN REAL ESTATE DEALS

If you are a real estate broker, contractor, builder or real estate attorney, you no doubt already contact some of the following people and sources in your daily work for commissions, fees and contracts. Whatever your occupation, if you are or want to be a successful real estate investor, it is most important that you know and utilize the following whole local community of people and organizations. (Key investing principles: know your area; know its people; look around; ask around.)

• *Town Water Commissioner.* Contact him for maps of water lines and particularly for any proposed new water districts or public water extensions. Current federal legislation and environmental policy are promoting and funding healthy community water supplies throughout our land. A spin-off of such activity is that land tracts and building lots alongside new water lines become much more valuable.

• *Town Sewer Official.* Contact him for information and maps similar to above. Federal legislation in its stress on clean water is also funding community sewer systems to curb pollution of water supplies. Land and building lots become even more valuable when they have water *and* sewer lines available. So go where the lines are going; invest in land and lots which are served or will be served by these lines. (See later chapters on land investments.)

• *Planning Officials.* The county planner has master plans that show projected growth areas. Local planning officials know and can tell you which sections of the community are proposed or approved for development.

• *Town Clerk.* This is where you get that all-important zoning ordinance and map—and where you keep up with new zoning changes which affect values.

• *Assessor.* He has confirmed property sale and description records, and has maps which can identify properties for you.

• *Building Inspector.* His records complement those of the other local officials and his building permit file shows where the building activity is.

• *Highway Engineer.* He can tell you where the new roads are going, when they are proposed to be built, which new interchanges are planned and where daily car counts are rising. All these factors can lead to high real estate profits from deals in affected properties.

• *Local newspaper.* Important sources for real estate sales ads, they also carry the small-type legal notices on foreclosures and lien sales. (See later chapter.) They report on meetings of local planning officials and boards where development actions are taken. They report when and where new industries are being located. Local newspapers should be read carefully. They report on all happenings that affect local people and property.

• *Surveyors.* They are always a good source for investors who want to cash in on local real estate profit opportunities.

• *Contractors.* Also often good sources for leads on good real estate investments.

• *Title Searchers.* Have an overview position on real estate activity in their area.

• *Engineers and Architects.* Often have excellent information on what's happening in their areas and where the good deals are.

• *Real Estate Brokers.* These people are of course a basic source.

• *Attorneys.* Particularly those attorneys who specialize in real estate or estates, often have leads on good properties for investment.

• *Bank Officials.* Loan officers in banks not only have data on real estate in their area, but also often have foreclosed houses for sale.

• *Park Commissioners.* Property alongside new or proposed parks usually becomes more valuable.

• *Local Merchants.* Businessmen in an area are not only a good

information source. They also often have surplus funds for investment
in local real estate deals.

• *Utility Officials.* Utilities keep records of real estate activity and
growth areas.

AN OVERALL REAL ESTATE DATA RESOURCES
GUIDE

The real estate data resources guide (opposite) summarizes in
checklist form all these information aids and sources:

A Case History of Big Local Turnaround Profits

As an informed local person, you are right there to spot and
invest in turnaround real estate opportunities. You're on the local
ground, the first to see local neighborhood or economic conditions
and property values beginning to change. In one depressed real estate
Northeast county, an alert real estate broker I know recently bought
105 acres of farmland 70 miles from New York City for $300 an acre.
This land and similar properties had been selling for ten times as
much during a land boom five years earlier. As population from the
metropolis pressed northward again, this broker-developer subdivided the farmland into its zoned segments of residential, commercial and industrial plottage. The land is now again valued and being
sold at $2500 per acre in acreage plots and $16,500 per half-acre
building plot—a profit saga based on informed local investment in
our changing real estate scene. It also shows a successful local investor alert to local conditions who kept up with regional and national
economic and real estate trends impacting his local area.

HOW YOU CAN TRADE IN YOUR LOCAL
KNOWLEDGE AND CONTACTS
FOR BIG REAL ESTATE PROFITS

How many times have you heard a neighbor or other local
person "put down" your local area? "Why, I remember when that
property could have been bought for $20,000 and now they want
$80,000!" Or, "They'll never get their money back on that land. It was
offered to me for half last year and I thought it was too high then!"

Somehow, the other man's grass is always greener or sup-
posedly more valuable. Familiarity with one's own local area often

REAL ESTATE
DATA RESOURCES GUIDE

<u>Aids</u>
- ____ Topographic Map file
- ____ Zoning Ordinance
- ____ Zoning Map
- ____ Building Ordinance
- ____ Community Master Plan
- ____ Sewer Map
- ____ Public Water Map
- ____ Parks Map
- ____ Local Newspapers
- ____ Local Assessor Tax Maps
  which locate properties

<u>Local Officials</u>
- ____ Assessor
- ____ Highway Engineer
- ____ Town Clerk
- ____ Building Inspector
- ____ Water Commissioner
- ____ Sewer Commissioner
- ____ Planning Officials

<u>Professionals</u>
- ____ Surveyors
- ____ Architects
- ____ Engineers
- ____ Title Searchers
- ____ Attorneys
- ____ Real Estate Brokers
- ____ Banks

<u>Other</u>
- ____ Local Merchants
- ____ Chamber of Commerce
- ____ Utility Officials
- ____ Banks
- ____ Local friends, neighbors
  & relatives

<u>U.S. Government Agencies</u>
- ____ Dept of Census
- ____ Housing & Urban Development (HUD)
- ____ Veterans Administration (VA)
- ____ Superintendent of Documents, U.S. Govt Printing Office
- ____ Dept of Commerce
- ____ Environmental Protection Agency (EPA)
- ____ Farmers Home Administration (FmHA)
- ____ Dept. of Army Engineer Corps
- ____ Small Business Administration (SBA)
- ____ General Services Administration (GSA)
- ____ Library of Congress

<u>State Agencies</u>
- ____ Economic Development Agencies
- ____ Departments of Labor
- ____ State Planning Commissioners
- ____ State Dept. of Commerce

<u>Other</u>
- ____ Libraries
- ____ Trade Associations

does breed contempt for its value potential. A human failing perhaps, but one that can cost you money if you are not objective.

So you don't have to journey afar to find the action. It's going on wherever you are locally and much more is coming your way.

Where you live or work can be your real estate gold mine. To get the gold out from unusual, local real estate deals, you not only have to be on the spot but you also have to know what to do. The following six-part guidance procedure outlines how you trade in your local knowledge and contacts safely and profitably for real estate profits:

1. *Invest within your local sphere of knowledge and activity.* This does not mean that you have to be limited to the neighborhood where you live. Your local investment area includes the entire territory where you live, work or travel fairly regularly for business and/or pleasure. Distance is not the only yardstick; local knowledge, contacts and regular, *personal* presence in the investment area are what pay off.

2. *Develop your local investment sources.* Whether broker, merchant, banker, neighbor, tax lien or foreclosure publications, cultivate and expand such sources. Local newspapers are also often gold mines of real estate leads—not just for their real estate ads but also for the legal notices and local news events affecting real estate. For example, when a local newspaper recently published a foreclosure notice by a local bank, I bid in and bought the property at an extremely low price. The same local bank later helped refinance the property after the sale and we were able to resell the property subject to the new mortgage for an excellent profit.

3. *Be alert to new profit opportunities.* Is a new industry coming to town which will affect values? A new road? Are turnaround real estate situations developing? A canny investor I know noticed the A&P supermarket in his town closing down and converting to a subsidiary discount food store. He followed up quickly on this new marketing trend and now owns and leases three discount food chain stores to the A&P in his region.

4. *Watch for new investment concepts.* Are new real estate ideas, originated elsewhere, applicable to your area? For instance, would a mini-warehouse go? Does your area have many apartment dwellers concentrated within a two-mile distance? Mini-warehouses could be most profitable in such locations.

5. *Be alert to new laws.* These new laws can make money for you locally. For example, is there a historical section in your community where you could buy up properties cheaply? There are various national and state laws which encourage the restoration of such historical properties through generous tax breaks.

6. *Watch the growth patterns.* You're in the best local position to know what's happening locally. Is the boom coming to your area or other sections you know? What's happening with building permits?

Are certificates of occupancy increasing? This is probably one of the most important guidelines. If you invest in the path of growth, you're bound to make money. When you see building subdivisions being approved along a major road, you can surely anticipate that adjacent land tracts or smaller, bypassed parcels will become more valuable. When new industries move into an area, the surrounding industrial and commercial land booms in value. Be alert to trends. Is it time to jump into minor land subdivisions, into buy-up, fix-up real estate deals?

WHEN TO GET INTO LOCAL REAL ESTATE
MINI-SYNDICATES

Do-it-yourself real estate investing or pooling your investment funds with a few people locally in a small mini-syndicate group differs markedly from typical large-scale real estate limited partnerships. In limited partnership investing, you depend completely on the reputation, knowledge and experience of the professional manager who is the general partner. You are the limited partner. The general partner always gets paid for his work first and also gets a larger share of any profits. A minimum of 10% right off the top is customary. The law requires that you get a prospectus before you invest in such limited partnerships, but no law guarantees profits for all these fees and percentages you pay.

If you want to invest in your area but have limited cash, try joining up with other local persons in small investment groups of no more than three to five people. These "mini-syndicates," if kept small to permit easier decision-making, usually produce more return for their members than the large professional syndicators who often produce only their own fees. For safety, stick to those you know. Try to go in with real estate brokers, surveyors, lawyers, merchants, knowledgeable local people or a property owner who may want to develop his property.

HOW YOU'RE IN THE BEST LOCAL POSITION
TO GET PROPERTY AND OTHER TAX BREAKS

Land value goes up and down depending on a variety of location, growth pattern, inflation and regional-local economic factors. However, the long range trend of land value is up . . . some economists calculate an average of 10% per year in recent decades. As in all real estate investment, however, investment in land for value appreciation cannot be made with only an eye on statistical averages.

Land investment must be based on an informed objective market analysis of all factors, particularly current and projected local market conditions.

Once this market analysis is done and the land purchased, there are ways to hold down your carrying costs while you hold onto the land for long-term increase in value and capital appreciation. Carrying costs on vacant land fall into two categories:

1. *Principal and interest payments* on the mortgage you give to a bank or to the seller when you buy the land. Although some people buy land for cash, professional investors always try to pay little or no cash down so that the later land value appreciation and capital gain profits when sold will be based mainly on the borrowed money or "leverage" rather than just on their own smaller total of cash investment. These "P and I" costs are reduced and other income sheltered because you get income tax deductions for the interest you pay but not for the principal. So it pays also to arrange for low principal payments when you buy the land. This is often possible, particularly if you are known locally.

2. *Property Taxes.* Here is where you are in the best position locally to get property taxes on the land reduced while you wait for the land to go up in value. Many states offer property tax exemptions to those landowners who farm their land or keep their land forested. You are in the best position locally to arrange for locally managed or tenanted farming on your land or to arrange for tree planting (often state subsidized) and then apply for these property tax exemptions which are substantial. For example, one local businessman I know, who also owns a nearby 100-acre tract, keeps a small herd of beef cattle on his land. With the high price of beef lately, he only has to buy or sell about six cows each year in order to meet the requirements of doing a minimum $10,000 annual "farm" business to qualify for tax exemptions. He saves thousands of dollars annually in property taxes while the land keeps increasing in value. These state property tax exemptions do vary widely so you should contact your state property tax officer for local details. (See full 50-state address list which follows.)

A 50-STATE ADDRESS LIST
OF STATE TAX OFFICIALS

Chief, Ad Valorem Tax Division Alabama Dept. of Revenue Montgomery, Alabama 36102	Director, Div of Property and Special Taxes Dept of Revenue Phoenix, Arizona 85038
State Assessor, Dept of Commerce & Reg Affairs, Div of Local Govt Assessment, PO Box 710 Juneau, Alaska 99801	Director, Assessment Coord. Div—Dept. of Comm.—Exec Bldg—2020 W 3rd St Little Rock, Arkansas 72205

Chief, Div of Assessment Stds State Bd of Equalization PO Box 1799 Sacramento, Calif 95808	Director, Property Tax Division Iowa Dept of Revenue Lucas State Office Bldg Des Moines, Iowa 50319
Property Tax Administrator Dept Local Affairs—Propty Tax 614 Capitol Annex Denver, Colorado 80203	Director, Div Propty Val—Dept of Revenue—State Office Bldg Topeka, Kansas 66612
Municipal Assessment Agent State Tax Dept 92 Farmington Ave Hartford, Connecticut 06115	Director, Property & Inheritance Tax Div—Kentucky Dept of Revenue State Capitol, Frankfort, Ky 40601
Director, Div of Revenue State Dept of Finance 601 Delaware Avenue Wilmington, Del 19899	Chairman, Louisiana Tax Commission PO Box 44244—Capitol Station Baton Rouge, Louisiana 70804
Director, Ad Valorem Tax Bureau, State Dept Revenue Room 230 Carlton Bldg Tallahassee, Florida 32304	State Tax Assessor—Bur of Taxation State Office Bldg Augusta, Maine 04330
Director of Equalization Georgia Dept of Revenue Trinity Washington Bldg Atlanta, Georgia 30334	Deputy Director—Dept of Assessment & Tax—301 West Preston St Baltimore, Maryland 21201
Asst Director—Tax Property Technical Office Hawaii Dept of Taxation PO Box 259 Honolulu, Hawaii 96809	Associate Commissioner—Div of Local Finance— Dept of Corp & Tax 100 Cambridge St Boston, Mass 02204
State Tax Commission Property Division, PO Box 36 Boise, Idaho 83722	Executive Secretary, State Tax Comm Dept of Treasury—Treasury Bldg Lansing, Michigan 48922
Director, Dept of Local Gov Affrs State of Illinois 303 E Monroe St Springfield, Illinois 62706	Director, Propty Equalization Div State Dept of Tax, Centennial Office Bldg, St. Paul, Minnesota 55145
Chairman, State Bd Tax Commissioners State Office Bldg—Rm 201 Indianapolis, Indiana 46204	Ad Valorem Commissioner State Tax Commission PO Box 960 Jackson, Mississippi 39205

Chairman, State Tax Comm
State Capitol
Jefferson City, Mo. 65101

Assessment Supvsr—Office
State Tax
Commissioner—State Capitol
Bismarck, North Dakota 58501

Director, Propty Tax Field
Program—Dept of Revenue
Mitchell Bldg
Helena, Montana 59601

Chief, Propty Tax Div—Ohio Tax
Dept—PO Box 530
Columbus, Ohio 43216

Administrator, Propty Tax Div
Dept of Revenue, PO Box 94818
Lincoln, Nebraska 68509

Director, Ad Valore Division
Oklahoma Tax Commission
2101 Lincoln Blvd
Oklahoma City, Oklahoma
73194

Director, Div of Assessment
Stds
Dept of Tax
Carson City, Nevada 89701

Administrator, Assessment &
Appraisal Div—Oregon
Dept of Rev
504 State Office Bldg
Salem, Oregon 97310

Secretary, Dept of Revenue
Administration, State Office
Bldg
Concord, New Hampshire
03301

Chairman, State Tax
Equalization Board—Box 1294
Harrisburg, Pennsylvania 17108

State Supervisor, Local
Property
& Public Utility Branch
Div of Tax—Dept of Treasury
West State & Will
Trenton, New Jersey 08625

Supervisor, Tax Equalization Sect
Dept of Community Affairs
150 Washington St
Providence, R.I. 02808

Director, Property Tax Dept
Bataan Memorial Bldg
Santa Fe, New Mexico 87503

Director, Propty Tax Div—State
Tax Commission—Box 125
Columbia, S.C. 29214

Director, State Bd Equalization
& Assessment—Agency Bldg
Empire State Plaza
Albany, NY 12223

Propty Tax Div—State Dept
Revenue
State Capitol Bldg
Pierre, S.D. 57501

Secretary, State Bd Assessment
Dept of Revenue, PO Box 25000
Raleigh, North Carolina 27640

Director, Div Propty
Assessment
Office State Comptroller
289 Plus Park Blvd
Nashville, Tennessee 37217

Director, Ad Valorem Tax Div
Comptroller of Public Accounts
State of Texas—Capitol Bldg
Austin, Texas 78711

Asst Dir, Propty Taxes—State
Dept of Revenue—General
Adm Bldg
Olympia, Washington 98504

Director, Local Value Div—State
Tax Comm—2870 Connor St
Salt Lake City, Utah 84109

Dir, Local Govt Relations Division
State Tax Dept, 301 Capitol Bldg
Charleston, West Virginia 25305

Property Tax Division—Dept of
Taxes—State Office Bldg
Montpelier, Vt. 05602

Dir, Propty & Utility Tax Bureaus
Dept Revenue—1000 State
Office Bldg
Madison, Wisconsin 53702

State Tax Commissioner, Dept
of Tax—P.O. Box 6-L
Richmond, Virginia 23215

Dir, Ad Valorem Tax
Dept—Dept Revenue
& Tax—2200 Carey Av
Cheyenne, Wyoming 82002

Assessment Stds
Specialist—Dept
Finance & Rev—Rm
4126—Muncipal Center 300
Indiana Av, NW
Washington, DC 20001

4

Little-Known
Real Estate Financing
and Tax Break Techniques

This chapter deals with money, that most important investment tool. It stresses money of others, not yours. That favorite word of professional investors, *leverage*, is shown to be simply a way to use other people's money to pyramid your profits. There is an equally important section on how to keep most of your real estate profits by getting big tax credits under new little-known tax laws for commercial and industrial renovations. Specific little-known real estate financing alternatives are developed in detail, including how to invest and get loans during tight-money times . . . when to assume mortgages . . . when to use contract-sale techniques . . . when to utilize second mortgages . . . how to avoid personal liability. All the various conventional places and ways to borrow money as well as definitions of important loan terminology are listed for your ready reference. Techniques are also spelled out on how to cut the ever-increasing costs of loan closing.

HOW TO INCREASE YOUR PROFITS
BY USING OTHER PEOPLE'S MONEY

The arithmetic of investing and of leverage is simple. If you use your *own* money only for 100% of the purchase price of a real estate investment, your profit is figured as a percentage of your investment.

Thus, if you buy a property for $50,000, pay cash and sell it for $60,000, you have made $10,000 or a 20% return on your investment before expenses. However, if you bought the same property for $10,000 cash with balance financed by a $40,000 mortgage, the same $60,000 sale would have given you a 100% return on your investment! Your only additional expense would have been the interest you had to pay on the mortgage before you sold the property.

You don't have to be rich to get richer in real estate. Money often helps move along deals quickly but uninformed hasty investment often loses this investment money instead of making profits. Using other people's money wisely to make money is the name of the game in real estate.

HOW TO GET UNUSUAL, BIG TAX BREAKS FROM COMMERCIAL AND INDUSTRIAL RENOVATIONS

The secret ingredient of making money in real estate is threefold. First, you have to get to the profitable investment before others do. Second, you have to get good financing terms. Third, you have to know how to keep most of your real estate profits from being paid out in taxes so that you can use these profits to find and fund other profitable, little-known investments. This is known as "pyramiding," getting rich in real estate, etc.

Recent tax laws have generally tended to restrict more and more investment fields which were used to shelter or protect income—except in real estate. If anything, real estate has not only become one of the few remaining tax shelter investments; it has been made even more attractive.

The Revenue Act of 1978 closed many tax loopholes but also opened new profit vistas for real estate investments. Its provisions are pervasive and critically important. These little-known new provisions affect all of the later sections in this book which deal with any type of commercial or industrial property renovated and held for investment. For individual legal advice or other expert assistance on your own tax considerations involved in such real estate, you should consult your own tax attorney and accountant. Generally, in terms of impact on real estate investment, the following factors are new and important:

1. *Capital gains deduction* is increased from 50% to 60% of the net capital gain. Thus, if there is a $10,000 net profit, only $4000 is now taxable.

2. *"At risk" rules* have been extended to all activities other than real estate. A taxpayer in practically all activities can no longer deduct losses in excess of his actual economic investment—except to any partnership, the *principal activity of which is investing in real property* (other than mineral property). Thus, if a real estate property which includes a building on land valued at $25,000 is bought for $100,000 with $20,000 invested and the balance of $80,000 borrowed by mortgage, then the full $75,000 of buildings can continue to be depreciated even though only $20,000 of your own money is at risk. Practically no other investment can do this now.

3. *Investment tax credits* of up to 10% and $100,000 limitation on used property have been made permanent—and extended to rehabilitation or renovation of buildings used for trade or business, such as factories, warehouses, hotels, retail and wholesale stores and historic structures under certain conditions. Buildings have to have been in use for *at least 20 years* and rehabilitation can be done only once every 20 years. Interior and exterior rehab costs are eligible. If more than 25% of exterior walls are replaced, then costs will not qualify. Rehabilitation items must have a useful life of at least five years. Such properties have to be held for more than seven years to get the benefit of the full 10% tax credit; if held for five to seven, then 6.66 tax credit. If held for less than five years, the full tax credit has to be recaptured.

4. *An example of a tax credit.* It is important to understand that this is a full tax credit, not just a deduction. The amount comes right off the top of the full tax due. Thus, say a 30-year-old industrial building is purchased and converted from former manufacturing use to warehouse use by closing up windows, installing loading docks, overhead doors and office space. The building is purchased for $100,000 with $30,000 ascribed to the land. Conversion costs are $200,000. The investment tax credit would probably be $20,000 which would be fully deducted from the property owner's total tax due for that year. In addition, the property owner could also depreciate the original building cost of $70,000 plus the renovation cost of $200,000. If the property is sold after eight years, the investment tax credit *does not* have to be recaptured in any part.

HOW TO GET MORTGAGES, EVEN DURING TIGHT MONEY TIMES

We learn from history. Whenever interest rates went up, people pulled their money out of savings accounts to buy higher interest treasury bills and other higher-yield instruments. This "disintermediation," as it is called in financial circles, caused "tight money" markets because banks had less money for real estate mortgage lending. The federal government has since then utilized agencies like Federal National Mortgage, "Fannie May" (FNMA), now a private corporation, government subsidized, to buy up mortgages originated by banks, as a secondary lender, so as to keep banks liquid to make more loans. Although such government-aided efforts helped keep some mortgages flowing in the late-seventies interest surge, mortgage money still became harder to get and much more expensive.

When you invest in real estate you have to pick not only the place but also the time. A good buy may be a good buy mainly because it can't be sold readily due to a current tight money market for mortgages. This is when understanding, anticipating and capitalizing on prime rate interest effects on real estate activity pan out. If you see that the prime rate charged prime, big borrowing corporations is going up because the Federal Reserve is trying to control the money market, you know mortgage rates will soon be going up. This is when you should be trying to pin down lower interest mortgage commitments for investments you are planning before they go up. This is also when good buys become more available as tougher financing slows real estate activity. If you can't get mortgage terms and rates to your liking because of the tightening market, try asking the seller to take back a purchase money mortgage so that you can buy the property from him.

An Example of Financing During Tight Money Times

In 1974, as part of a small local syndicate of investors, I bought an 87-acre tract good for residential development for $2000 per acre. Mortgages could not be gotten then at any terms. Instead, the seller gave us an 80% purchase money mortgage for 20 years with the first five years set for interest payments only, then partial payments on principal plus interest for the remaining 15 years with a "balloon" principal payment to pay the balance at the end of the mortgage term. Interest was established at 1½% *below* the prevailing mortgage rates (if mortgages had been available) on the theory that the seller was not lending us hard cash as a bank would to buy his property. Instead, he was helping to create an 80% paper debt, based on the negotiated total value of the property with the property as security for the purchase money mortgage he took back from us. A spin-off benefit from this type of mortgage was that we had practically no closing costs to pay on this deal (which we sold two years later for $3300 per acre).

WHEN TO ASSUME A MORTGAGE AND WHEN TO USE CONTRACT SALES

During such tight money times, another financing avenue is to assume an existing mortgage. This means that you buy a property by assuming or taking over its mortgage obligation. There are various ways to do this, such as making it subject to the mortgage or "assuming" it. This should be done only on advice of your attorney and only after all the terms and obligations of the existing mortgage are carefully reviewed and understood. It is one way of making a real estate deal work when a new mortgage can't be originated or if a new mortgage is uneconomical. Sometimes the existing mortgage is better. It also saves closing costs.

Contract sale or installment sale is another little-known method of transferring property. Usually it's better to *sell* a property by contract or installment sale rather than to buy it this way. This is because the contract buyer does not get a deed; usually he does not own the property until he pays in a certain agreed-upon percentage of the purchase price. However, in tight money times, this is another alternative way to buy the good deals which usually become available during such times. Similar techniques like *option-purchase* and *lease with option to buy* can also be used to tie up and cash in on good deals. In all such cases, be guided by your attorney in making certain that your contract or option interest in the property is legally vested in you.

SECOND MORTGAGES: HOW TO MAKE THE MOST OF THEM

When an area is in growth or even in an explosive real estate value spiral like in the Southwest recently, second mortgages become a good deal. The home or property owner can find ready cash by giving a second mortgage on his property. People who invest in mortgages can lend money then on second mortgages with comparative safety. If you invest in property, a second mortgage becomes a good tool for buying and selling in such growth areas. It often makes possible the takeover of existing mortgages so that the buyer needs less cash and the seller becomes able to sell his property.

How a Second Mortgage Helped Earn a $113,000 Profit

In the prior example of the 87-acre farm bought for $2000 per acre and sold for $3300 per acre, we made the sale possible by taking back a second mortgage for $105,000. The buyer who bought the property from us assumed the existing first mortgage which had been created when we bought the property. The arithmetic for this resale went as follows:

Purchase Price—87 Acres @ $3300 = $287,100
Cash Payment ....(15%) = $43,100
Assume Existing 1st Mortgage...................................139,000
2nd Mortgage 105,000

Total...$287,100
(Gross Profit—$113,000!)

It is also important whenever you buy property to let the property—and not your own pocketbook—be the security for the mortgage you give! You should avoid personally guaranteeing the mortgage bond or debt. If the property is not good security for the mortgage, you probably should not be buying it anyhow. In any event, a real estate investor's cardinal rule should always be to let each deal stand by itself. Lenders like to get all the security they can for a mortgage. Investors must avoid pledging their personal assets. In all investments, read and have your lawyer review the fine print in the mortgage terms to make certain that you are relieved from personal liability.

ALL THE PLACES TO GET FINANCING

Using other people's money is the way to real estate fortunes. Who has this money? The following is a reference list of conventional as well as little-known sources of money.

WHERE TO GET MONEY

Conventional Mortgages from Institutions

1. Savings Banks
2. Commercial Banks
3. Savings and Loan Associations
4. Building and Loan Associations
5. Title and Trust Companies
6. Mortgage bankers who represent individuals, banks, insurance companies or other institutional lenders.

Government-Backed Mortgages from Institutions

1. V.A. guaranteed loans for veterans' housing
2. F.H.A.-H.U.D. insured housing loans

Direct Government Loans to Purchasers

1. V.A. loans to all people who buy VA-foreclosed properties.
2. F.H.A. loans to all people who buy FHA-foreclosed properties.
3. S.B.A. business loans
4. Farmers Home Administration housing and other loans

Other and Little-Known Ways to Raise Money

1. *Assume* an existing mortgage.
2. *Second mortgages* from lending institutions.
3. *First and second mortgages* from individuals.
4. *Purchase money* mortgages from sellers.
5. *Graduated payment mortgages* from banks to young people with good economic potential.
6. *Reverse annuity mortgages* from banks permitting older people to borrow against rising equity in their property to meet costs of rising taxes and maintenance.
7. *Variable rate mortgages* from banks tailored to meet inflation by permitting the interest rate on a mortgage to move up and down.
8. *Mortgages from builders* who want to sell their buildings.
9. *Construction mortgages* from banks and other lenders.
10. *Installment or contract sales.*
11. *Options to purchase.*
12. *Leases with options* to purchase.
13. *Mortgages with special terms* like "interest only."
14. *Local syndication.*

These are all the usual and not-so-usual ways and places to get money. The documents involved in getting mortgage money for properties you own or purchase are as follows:

- *The note or bond* is the promise to pay and the document that sets forth the amount of the loan and conditions.
- *The mortgage* ("deed of trust" in California) is the document that pledges the property to secure the promise to pay and sets forth the conditions of the pledge and also gives the lender the power to acquire the property if the loan is not paid.
- *The deed* to the property is the written evidence of ownership and should be recorded by the county register of deeds.
- *The certification or opinion of title* assures that title is in your name, is clear or "marketable," that no one else has claim to the property except you.

HOW TO CUT HIGH CLOSING COSTS

Recent government surveys show spectacular increase in closing costs, the amount you have to pay in cash mainly for the lender's "expenses of closing" the mortgage (giving you the borrowed money). It is just as important to reduce these skyrocketing cash closing costs as it is to get the best mortgage terms possible. While you're shopping for a mortgage to reduce the total amount of your own cash which you have to invest, you can't afford to disregard these incidental closing costs. These surveys indicate that these costs are no longer so incidental and range up to about 6% of the purchase price.

For example, if you buy a property for $60,000 and are successful in arranging a $50,000 mortgage, you would have to pay $10,000 cash down payment plus up to an additional $3600 in cash for these closing costs. Most of these closing costs are figured as a percentage of your mortgage amount. In addition, many lenders, particularly mortgage banker companies, charge two to eight "points" depending on how tight the mortgage market is and how much they are paying to borrow their funds. These "points" are also charged as a percentage of the total mortgage amount so that total closing costs plus points can total up to, say, 13% of the purchase price.

These closing costs and points can typically involve the following charges on a $60,000 property purchase:

Survey	$150
Title insurance for bank	326
Legal fees and your title policy	750
Insurance premium and your credit report	425
Lawyer for bank and bank appraisal	300
Mortgage insurance	1100
Advance on real estate taxes	400
Bank filing fee	100
Deed and mortgage preparation	50
Points (6)	3000
TOTAL	$6601

The Real Estate Settlement Procedures Act, administered by the Federal Trade Commission and often studied by Housing and Urban Department (HUD) surveys, basically requires that bankers give buyers an information booklet shortly before the closing which states what these costs will be at closing. The fine print in these booklets is confusing, the information comes just before closing when it's too late to do anything about it anyway, and it hasn't helped to hold down these galloping closing cost increases at all.

STRATEGIES FOR CUTTING CLOSING COSTS

It's important to shop for lower closing costs, the same as you shop for mortgage amounts and terms. Some guidelines:

• Don't let yourself be steered by a broker. Reserve the right to pick your own lender, title company, attorney, escrow company, etc. Ask why a particular lender or company is recommended.

- Negotiate with the seller to pick up some or all of the closing costs.
- Don't be bashful about discussing fees with the lawyer you hire.
- Shop around for both mortgage terms *and* closing costs and points. Get all charges itemized in advance. Excessive closing costs and points at one lender can negate attractive lower down payment requirements and interest rates.
- If you assume an existing mortgage, give a purchase money mortgage or get a direct government mortgage, you can cut out practically all of these closing costs.

5

How to Avoid the Pitfalls of Unusual Real Estate Investment Opportunities

Your goal in real estate investment is to make money, plenty of money . . . not to lose your investment. The whole thrust of this chapter is to show all the ways to maximize these little-known local real estate profit opportunities and still minimize the risks. To do this, you are shown first how to appraise real estate using the market approach and other modern valuation techniques. Then there is a section on how to buy at market or below and still avoid "sucker-bait" bargains. Techniques are detailed here on how to negotiate local real estate deals and how to use leverage (borrowed funds) without personal guaranty. You are also shown how to spot and bypass those real estate investments where development may be blocked by no-growth, zoning, environmental and flood-plain control restriction. Finally, there is a checklist of the nine biggest pitfalls in real estate investing and how to avoid them.

HOW TO MAKE SURE YOU'RE GETTING GOOD VALUE

To profit from real estate you have to buy and sell right. Even if you hire professional appraisers to advise you, you have to understand and act on their reports properly. In the final analysis, it's *your* investment money, *your* total analysis of the proposition, *your* local knowledge of the deal—and *your* decision. Modern appraisal tools make such decisions feasible.

Whether you want to determine if you're buying at or below market or selling for the right price and profit, you have to know the property's value. There are many "faces" of value. For instance, there is *insurance value* to the insured and to the insurance companies, who are both concerned with how much it costs to *replace* destroyed property. There is *amenity value* which is a nice general term appraisers assign usually to residences to cover those value factors which don't produce economic return like rent, yet make for pleasurable living. There is *salvage value* when we junk building improvements for cash and so on.

However, there is only one value that most investors in real estate are concerned with, and that is *market value*. Whether vacant land or built-on land, property gets its value from what people will pay for it or for *similar* properties, similarly situated—otherwise known as *comparable* properties. Even when you buy apartment houses or commercial or industrial property where the return on investment is what attracts the investment, you must check the market to see what similar properties are selling for. I've often seen investors run down a rent roll to the bottom line and buy based on the alleged return without checking the validity of the roll or what similar buildings sold for.

This market approach has become the best approach to value for practically all residential vacant land and many other properties as our society has become more suburbanized. We now have massive "comparable" sales of similar properties, similarly situated, sold daily almost everywhere. Sources for such comparable data include real estate brokers, assessors, lawyers, title companies and neighbors. The step-by-step technique is simple and methodical.

THREE KEY STEPS
TO MARKET VALUE

Step 1—Keep your comparable sales of similar properties *close to subject* in terms of price, date of sale, similar improvements and similar location.

Step 2—*Use three to five comparable sales* for your analysis but *don't average* them to get the appraised value of the property you're appraising. Study these sales and adjust them by their various attributes as they compare to the subject. In most cases you'll finally come to an informed opinion that one or two of the comparables are the "best comparables" and the others support your conclusion.

Step 3—Finally, set down your opinion of value in dollars for subject property.

The completed FNMA Appraisal Report shown in Figure 5-1 is a good example of such an analysis of comparable data for the market approach to value on residential property. This form also contains an example of cost approach for the same property. (See page 64.)

HOW TO USE
THE INCOME APPROACH

The *income approach* is generally used for commercial properties to determine what a property is worth based on the income it produces. It is an appraisal technique which uses the expected net income from a property to determine how much investment is needed to produce this net income. This capital amount of investment is actually the present value of the property since investors normally purchase commercial properties for a return on their investment. This following step-by-step procedure is involved:

Step 1. Net income is secured by deducting vacancy percentage (usually 5% to 10%) and operating expenses like insurance, taxes, maintenance, fuel, utilities, management from the *gross income* flowing from the building and land. (Gross income should be checked by market approach if figures can be obtained by comparing it with similar properties.)

Step 2. Rate of capitalization is then determined. There are various ways to do this. The best way is to analyze sales of similar properties, but this data is often hard to find. There are alternative ways. One way is to *"build up" a rate*. For example, since we are involved with investment, we can use "safe" current bond rates—say 8%—then add 1% *each* for management, non-liquidity and risk to give a total 11% capitalization rate for the subject property. Or another way is to use a *"band of investment"* technique. Thus, if there is a 60% first mortgage available for the property @ 9½% and a 40% owner's equity estimated @ 9%, then 60% @ 9½% plus 40% @ 9% plus a recapture rate of 2% on a 50-year economic life for the property would give 5.7% + 3.6% + 2% = 11.3% capitalization rate.

The following is an example of income approach calculation using *band of investment* technique. (First mortgage 60% @ 9.5% or 5.7%. Equity 40% @ 9% or 3.6% plus 40-year economic life or 2½% = total capitalization rate of 11.8%.)

VALUATION SECTION

Purpose of Appraisal is to estimate Market Value as defined in Certification & Statement of Limiting Conditions (FHLMC Form 439/FNMA Form 1004B)., If submitted for FNMA, the appraiser must attach (1) sketch or map showing location of subject, street names, distance from nearest intersection, and any detrimental conditions and (2) exterior building sketch of improvements showing dimensions.

COST APPROACH

Measurements	No. Stories	Sq. Ft.
24 x 38' x 1 = 912		
2' x 21' x CANTILEVER = 42		
12' x 28' x FIN. BASEMENT = 336 (BELOW GRADE)		
x x =		
x x =		

Total Gross Living Area (List in Market Data Analysis below) 954

Comment on functional and economic obsolescence: No GARAGE IN AREA WHERE GARAGES ARE STANDARD) ADVERSE VIEW OF RUNDOWN PROPERTY.

ESTIMATED REPRODUCTION COST — NEW — OF IMPROVEMENTS:

Dwelling 954 Sq. Ft. @ $ 27	=	$ 24900
Sq. Ft. @ $	=	
Extras FIN. BASEMENT	=	
336 S.F. X 15.00	=	5000
CHAIN LINK FENCE	=	400
Porches, Patios, etc.	=	
Garage/Car Port ____ Sq. Ft. @ $	=	
Site Improvements (driveway, landscaping, etc.)	=	500
Total Estimated Cost New	=	$ 30800

Less	Physical	Functional	Economic		
Depreciation $ 3000	$	$1000	=	$ (4000)

Depreciated value of improvements	=	$ 26800
ESTIMATED LAND VALUE	=	$ 11500
(If leasehold, show only leasehold value)		
INDICATED VALUE BY COST APPROACH		$ 38300

The undersigned has recited three recent sales of properties most similar and proximate to subject and has considered these in the market analysis. The description includes a dollar adjustment, reflecting market reaction to those items of significant variation between the subject and comparable properties. If a significant item in the comparable property is superior to, or more favorable than, the subject property, a minus (-) adjustment is made, thus reducing the indicated value of subject; if a significant item in the comparable is inferior to, or less favorable than, the subject property, a plus (+) adjustment is made, thus increasing the indicated value of the subject.

MARKET DATA ANALYSIS

ITEM	Subject Property	COMPARABLE NO. 1		COMPARABLE NO. 2		COMPARABLE NO. 3	
Address	22 NEVERSINK Pl.	4 LINDEN DR SUBURBIA		21 BERRY LN. SUBURBIA		7 GARDNER ST. SUBURBIA	
Proximity to Subj.		SIM. DEVEL ½ MI So.		SIM. DEVEL. ½ MI. So.		ADJACENT- CORNER	
Sales Price	$	$ 40500		$ 42000		$ 38000	
Price/Living area	$ ⌀	$ 44 ⌀		$ 47 ⌀		$ 39 ⌀	
Data Source		BUYER		BUYER		BROKER	
	DESCRIPTION	DESCRIPTION	+(—)$ Adjustment	DESCRIPTION	+(—)$ Adjustment	DESCRIPTION	+(—)$ Adjustment
Date of Sale and Time Adjustment		7/1/79		8/5/79		8/10/79	
Location	FAIR	GOOD	-1000	FAIR		FAIR	
Site/View	FAIR	FAIR		GOOD		GOOD	-1000
Design and Appeal	FAIR	FAIR		FAIR		FAIR	
Quality of Const.	AV	AV.		AV		AV	
Age	20	18		22		20	
Condition	GOOD	GOOD		GOOD		FAIR	+1000
Living Area Room Count and Total	Total 7 B-rms 3 Baths 1½	Total 7 B-rms 3 Baths 1½		Total 7 B-rms 3 Baths 1½		Total 7 B-rms 3 Baths 1½	
Gross Living Area	954 Sq.Ft.	920 Sq.Ft.		900 Sq.Ft.	+1000	980 Sq.Ft.	
Basement & Bsmt. Finished Rooms	1+1 RANCH BASEMENT 336 S.F	HI RANCH BSMT 306 SF		HI RANCH BSMT 290 SF		HI RANCH BSMT 340 SF	
Functional Utility	FAIR	FAIR		FAIR		FAIR	
Air Conditioning	1 (WINDOW)	3 (WINDOW)	-500	CENTRAL A/C	-1000	1 (WINDOW)	
Garage/Car Port	NONE	1 (BUILT IN)	-500	2 B.I.	-1000	NONE	
Porches, Patio, Pools, etc.				GOOD LANDSCAPING	-500		
Other (e.g. fireplaces, kitchen equip., heating, remodeling)		FIREPLACE	-1000				
Sales or Financing Concessions							
Net Adj. (Total)		☐ Plus; ☒ Minus $ 3000		☐ Plus; ☒ Minus $ 4000		☐ Plus; ☐ Minus $ 0	
Indicated Value of Subject		$ 37500		$ 38000		$ 38000	

Comments on Market Data COMP. #3 "BEST COMPARABLE, SIZE, LOCATION, AMENITIES"

INDICATED VALUE BY MARKET DATA APPROACH	$ 38000
INDICATED VALUE BY INCOME APPROACH (If applicable) Economic Market Rent $ 325 /Mo. x Gross Rent Multiplier 120	= $ 39000

This appraisal is made ☒ "as is" ☐ subject to the repairs, alterations, or conditions listed below ☐ completion per plans and specifications.

Comments and Conditions of Appraisal: COST APPROACH IS UPPER LIMIT - INCOME APPROACH NOT PERTINENT, BECAUSE OF SCARCITY OF HOUSE RENTALS - MARKET APPROACH IS BEST APPROACH BASED ON ADEQUATE SALES ACTIVITY IN AREA - COMPARABLE No. 3

Final Reconciliation: IS "BEST COMPARABLE"

This appraisal is based upon the above requirements, the certification, contingent and limiting conditions, and Market Value definition that are stated in
☐ FHLMC Form 439 /FNMA Form 1004B filed with client _____ 5/15 19___ ☐ attached.
If submitted for FNMA, the report has been prepared in compliance with FNMA form instructions.

I ESTIMATE THE MARKET VALUE, AS DEFINED, OF SUBJECT PROPERTY AS OF 9/1 19___ to be $ 38000

Appraiser(s) John Doe   Review Appraiser (If applicable)

☒ Did ☐ Did Not Physically Inspect Property

REVERSE

FIGURE 5-1

Annual Net Income	$ 77,000
Less interest imputed to land ($100,000 @ 8%)	8,000
Balance imputed to building	69,000
Building Value $69,000 ÷ 11.8%	585,000
Add Land Value	100,000
Total	$685,000

THE COST APPROACH

There is still another appraisal technique, the *cost approach*, which is usually used for insurance value of properties and for those very rare occasions when market and/or income data is not available. It is also used by some appraisers as a check or upper limit on their market approach—usually a waste of time and the client's money.

The cost approach has an arithmetic basis. It estimates in some detail how much it would cost to replace the building being appraised, then depreciates these theoretical replacement costs for wear and tear, age, outmoded function, if any, and neighborhood adverse effects, if any. Land value (from market approach) is then added and the total appraised value emerges. It is an outmoded approach with great margin for error and little relationship to actual real estate market conditions and is a good approach to avoid if you want to avoid real estate losses. You should also beware of appraisal reports that use this cost approach primarily.

HOW TO GET
GOOD BUYS SAFELY

To make money in local real estate investments, you have to know the local market intimately. In most cases, you use the market approach to appraise the property you are considering. You do this to make certain you're not paying more than the market. You try to pay less than the market to increase your potential for later profit by negotiating a good deal now. You have to know a bargain when you see one by making a complete investigation and proper appraisal. Yet most important for the state of your pocketbook, you also have to be able to recognize "sucker-bait" bargains which look like bargains but are really pitfalls. Often, these "bargains" are priced below the market and look appealing—good on surface investigation yet cancerous underneath.

A "Good Buy" Which Resulted in a $20,000 Loss

For example, one investor I know snapped up for $50,000 a vacant house which was offered for $20,000 under the local market. He planned to paint the house and then make a quick $20,000 profit on resale. He was so taken with this prospect of quick profit that he failed to notice that there was an industrial type heavy-duty sump pump in the basement near one corner of the foundation wall. He assumed it was there for minor seasonal seepage. After he bought the house he discovered to his dismay that it was threatened by a serious hydrostatic water condition from a groundwater table level 18" higher than the basement floor. It seems the dwelling was built too low, in terms of basement floor elevation, during a five-year drought period. When normal rains came again, the water table rose higher than the basement floor. The heavy-duty sump pump was there because ordinary sump pumps had burned out from constant use. Not only that, but the powerful pump was pulling sand out from under the foundation footings. One whole corner of the foundation was on the verge of collapse. Eventually, at very heavy cost, the (finished) basement had to be filled in above the water table level and converted into a crawl space. This investor who had rushed in so quickly on this "good buy" finally came out of this deal very slowly with a net $20,000 *loss*.

To make money in real estate safely, you must be able to recognize the quality of the real estate. You have to know when to stay away from properties that are not economically feasible to build on or are not built properly. The Land Feasibility and Construction Checklist presented here (Figure 5-2) should help you avoid pitfall investment properties and invest in real estate that has market acceptability and value.

HOW TO NEGOTIATE LOCAL
REAL ESTATE DEALS

Sellers usually add on a percentage to allow for negotiation. Buyers make offers. A real estate broker often appears to act as a middleman to bring the seller and buyer together. Actually, by his calling, the broker is obligated to get the highest price possible for the seller if the seller is paying the broker his commission. So buyers who invest in real estate must make their own decisions, come to their own opinions of value and, in the final analysis, do their own negotiation. If a broker is involved, he must submit to the seller all offers you make.

Again, negotiation must be based on what the market says. Your

LAND FEASIBILITY
AND
CONSTRUCTION CHECKLIST

The Plot	Building Exterior	Building Interior
• Community facilities, schools?	• Worn roof?	• Safe stairs?
• Transportation?	• Worn flashing?	• No settlement?
• Area low, flood prone?	• Chimney mortar O.K.?	• Dry basement?
• Block ponding?	• Dry rot near grade?	• Adequate electric?
• Plot ponding?	• Caulking needed?	• Heating condition?
• Does lot need fill?	• Painting needed?	• Plumbing material, condition?
• Any subsidence?	• Doors, windows functioning?	• All walls plumb?
• Grades permit function?	• Positive grades away from building?	• Termite tubes damage?
• Traffic adverse for residential use?	• Water drains away from garage?	• Dry rot in framing?
• Not enough traffic for commercial?	• Roof line not "swayback"?	• Size of spaces adequate?
• Neighbors adverse, like junkyard?	• Crawl space vents?	• Width of doors, halls adequate?
• Zoning permits usage?	• Attic louvers?	• Layout functional?
• Usable yard areas?	• No trip hazards, walks?	• Enough windows?
• Plot setting acceptable?	• Exterior steps safe?	• Fireplace works?
• Erosion, stable soils?		• Interior finish acceptable?
• Any encroachments?		• Enough insulation?
• Access road public?		• Heating cost if electric heat?
		• Garages long enough?
		• Condition of condo common lands?
		• Condition of condo common improvements?

FIGURE 5-2: Land Feasibility and Construction Checklist

investigation and appraisal must be thorough before you submit your offer. Naturally, if the seller can increase his listing price by an amount for negotiation, you can reduce your offer amount by a percentage also. Yet the deal, as it is often said, must be good for both the seller and buyer for it to be consummated. Too low an offer will kill the deal. Too high will ruin your later profits.

PROVEN NEGOTIATION TECHNIQUES

1. Don't be carried away by speculative fever in boom situations. Base all negotiation and offers on the market. Overpaying for future hoped-for quick resale may only find you the last man on the totem pole.

2. Don't let your eagerness to buy or sell show.

3. Don't let your need to buy or sell show.

4. Do submit offers and replies to broker or lawyer if one is involved. Eagerness or pressures can be masked through such an intermediary.

5. Don't be in a rush. Our world is full of real estate investments. If this one gets away, you may be saving your money or property for a better future deal.

6. Sell when the price is right. As a seller, try not to wait for the last profit buck. The world of real estate is full of sellers who still own their properties and tell new prospects, "I could have sold for more last year." The investor who pyramids a real estate fortune is the one who sells when the price is right enough without waiting to make his whole fortune on this one deal. There are deals enough for pyramiding later. This is the name of the real estate game. In order to make and not lose money in real estate, you have to act when the time and price are right.

HOW TO "LEVERAGE" WITHOUT PERSONAL GUARANTY AND HOW TO AVOID TAX WIPE-OUT

It is said that given a long enough lever and a place to stand, you can move the world. Given enough "leverage," that real estate action term for mortgage funds to finance real estate investment, you can move into a world of real estate profits.

Chapter 4 lists all the known and little-known financing techniques. This section stresses avoidance of personal guaranties. Real estate investing uses vacant and improved property to make money from renting or reselling the property. You borrow money to buy or build on a property by taking out a mortgage. The lender uses the property as collateral or security for the mortgage in case you don't repay the mortgage. This is also called using money of others to leverage or increase your profits or income from the property.

You pay interest for this money of others. This interest becomes another expense which is deducted from gross rents or from gross resale of the property to figure your net profit. That's all this borrowed money should be. You should not get carried away with investing to the point where you personally guarantee a mortgage with your own personal assets—your own house, car, savings, etc. Lenders like to get all the security possible for a mortgage. This should be avoided studiously.

For example, say you buy a property with a market value of $100,000 and you borrow $60,000 on it to meet the purchase price. The lender is secure if you default and he has to sell off the property to get back his money.

Let the property be the security for the mortgage. If it is not good enough security, you probably shouldn't be buying it anyhow. And be sure to read and have your lawyer read carefully all the terms in mortgage papers to make certain you're not signing such personal liability clauses and that there are clear clauses that exculpate you, leaving you personally not liable.

HOW TO AVOID
TAX WIPE-OUT OF PROFITS

Tax wipe-out of real estate profits is another pitfall that must be avoided. These laws change regularly. Your lawyer and accountant must be consulted for advice on your tax liabilities. The following general tax considerations are what you must keep in mind when you invest if you want to keep profits from real estate.

1. The *leverage* or mortgaged funds you use are not only an expense on your real estate; this same interest expense is a very important income tax deduction.

2. Other *tax shelters* for income include recent tax credits for commercial/industrial renovations as well as no taxes at all on 60% of long-term capital gains (properties sold for profit after being held more than 12 months).

3. *Depreciation* on real estate buildings which are purchased with borrowed funds can still be taken on the full purchase amount including the borrowed money (less land value). This very important "shelter" under partnership rules is just no longer generally available except to real estate investors.

4. *Installment sales.* When you sell, you must be careful to take no more than 30% of the selling price in the year of sale and be certain to take the principal payments in two or more installments. This will enable you to defer paying tax on the entire profit from the sale in the year of sale. Also, if you hold the property for more than one year, the tax paid on each year's gain will be figured as a long-term capital gain at a reduced tax percentage.

HOW TO SPOT AND BYPASS
LAND BLOCKED BY RESTRICTIONS

Real estate is not immediately exchangeable as money is for services and products. Big profits can be made from property—if it can be developed, rented and/or held for increase and resold. However, to do this there must be a renter or buyer. There is no market if local regulations limit development on a "no- or slow-growth" basis or if federal, state and local laws bar development of low flood plains. This is when the property owner becomes the last man on the investment totem pole, unable to get off, unable to sell, watching his assets dwindle through taxes and expenses without hope of profitable development, function or resale.

These pitfall investments in slow-growth locations can be avoided if you touch all the pre-investment research bases. Plans like the Ramapo Plan, which started in Rockland County, N.Y. in the early 1970s, are being enacted into law in many communities. These slow-growth zoning and other restrictions generally severely limit residential, commercial and industrial developments to areas and facilities that have the utilities and facilities to handle and absorb the developments. Some call this confiscation without proper compensation but courts have generally upheld these types of slow-growth plans as a proper local community control function. Thus, if you buy a tract of land for development beyond sewer and water lines, you probably will be unable to subdivide and improve the land in some communities.

So . . . don't just look at the land, the property, the investment. Drop into the town hall and look at the zoning ordinance, the subdivision ordinance, the building code. Talk to the building inspector, the chairman of the planning board, the town board. Do this *before* you sign up to buy.

The same M.O. or mode of operation is used to check out environmental bars to development and real estate investment opportunities. As local communities have reacted to uncontrolled or only partly controlled growth, so also have environmental controls and concerns begun to inhibit development and real estate activity in certain locations. Real estate is still the biggest game in town. It's still the one big business where an individual, the little man, not just the big corporation, can make big bucks. It's just that modern *informed* real estate investment takes into account and avoids investing wherever modern environmental restrictions bar or severely limit development.

For example, until fairly recently, and still in many of their zoning maps and ordinances, local communities zoned all their low, wet, "waste" land for industry. It may still be on their maps but if you stop your research after you look at the map, your investment money will probably "drown" in these low lands. All the suburbs, the buildings and paving built since WWII have made many of these lowlands flood prone. The Federal National Flood Insurance program became law in the mid-seventies. It provides that no federal government loans may be made, guaranteed or insured when the property is located in an identified flood-prone area, unless the community has adopted effective land-use controls and the property is covered by flood insurance. Most communities are participating in this national flood control program. They bar new construction in strips as much as one-quarter mile wide on each side of streams. Wetlands, fresh water, tidal marshes and swamps will not be issued permits by the Environmental Protection Agency or state agencies for filling, draining or building. It pays to look before you leap to invest in low land. The following is a flood hazard checkout procedure:

Step 1. Check to see if the property is in a flood hazard area. Check with the local building inspector and/or town engineer. Look at his flood hazard maps or contact HUD, Federal Insurance Administration, Washington, D.C.

Step 2. Determine whether flood insurance is available. If you are buying an industrial or other existing building located on low land, ascertain whether the property is or can be covered by federal flood insurance, sold through local insurance brokers.

Step 3. Check out community land use controls. Contact local authorities and review their land use controls on wetlands.

In sum, you invest in real estate to make money, lots of money, not to lose your investment. The following checklist summarizes these pitfalls and the specific ways to avoid them:

THE NINE BIGGEST PITFALLS
IN REAL ESTATE INVESTING
AND HOW TO AVOID THEM

1. *Personal guaranty.* In practically all real estate investments, it doesn't pay to personally guarantee mortgages, even if it means you can't buy the property.
2. *Too much cash.* Proper real estate investment thrives and multiplies on borrowed money. Buying properties for all cash or mostly cash almost always means smaller returns on your investment. It often also means all your investment eggs are in one basket.
3. *Too little cash.* The cash you do invest should be money you don't need for other reasons since real estate is not usually immediately negotiable like stocks or diamonds.
4. *Undevelopable land.* No- and slow-growth suburban zoning regulations, flood-plain and other modern environmental legal bars to land development have to be checked out very carefully now before you put your money down.
5. *Tax Wipe-Out of profits.* The most successful real estate investor is the one who makes his profits and keeps most of them. Real estate is one of the few tax shelters left. The astute investor is also the one who hires an experienced tax attorney to advise him legally.
6. *Last investor on the totem pole.* The best way to avoid getting stuck with a property is to avoid being carried away by speculative fever in boom situations. If you overpay higher than current market value, hoping for quick resale in a rising market to bail you out, you may wind up last man on the totem pole, unable to sell when you're ready for profit.
7. *Bad location, poor construction.* The best way to stay out of such bad investments is to check out properties thoroughly *before* you buy. Watch out particularly when you are offered extraordinarily "good buys," priced far below market value.
8. *Paid too much.* The long-range trend of real estate values is generally up but you don't want to grow old while you wait for profits. Proper appraisal is the way to go in real estate investment.
9. *Distant ownership.* One of the biggest pitfalls is absentee ownership because you're not there to analyze and keep up with what's going on with your investment. The way to avoid such problems is to invest locally.

6

How to Uncover Hidden Profit Opportunities in Land for Residential Development

Here is where the real wealth lies—in land and in the profits from its sale-resale, subdivision, development and improvement. Initial sections in this chapter show you how to find and profit from land tract deals and how to spot where sewer/water utilities and road changes will skyrocket land values. A companion section details techniques for discovering zoning changes—lake "gores" and abandoned rights-of-way—which bring big profits. You're also shown how land annexation techniques and "scattered" lot investment can produce high profits without big up-front cash investment. There are other sections on how to profit from and find land zoned for mobile homes, "clustering," planned unit development and condominiums.

LAND, THE ULTIMATE SOURCE OF WEALTH AND PROFITS

Land is the basis of all value. Since time immemorial, man has always bought and sold land and measured real wealth in terms of land ownership and usage. Most people appear to have a basic elemental urge to own land. There is always, in good or bad real estate times, an underlying market for land. Often, economic cyclical swings cause price fluctuation up and down, depending on location, but in general the long-range trend is always up. It is a *non-renewable* asset. As it is subdivided, improved, built on, no other land is created to take its vacant place. Land is a finite resource. Increasing population and expanding suburbs put even greater economic pressures and value on remaining developable land.

Examples of Skyrocketing Land Values

One out of every twelve Americans owns either a vacant recreational lot or a second home. This is only one startling example of Americans' hunger for land.

Not only our own countrymen but also thousands of wealthy foreign investors have been rushing to American shores to buy up farmland and other real estate.

Land is a hedge against inflation. Average land values have risen at far faster rates and to higher plateaus than even our galloping inflation. Not too long ago, for example, you could buy a house on its landscaped lot in Palos Verdes, California for what you have to pay for a *vacant* lot there now. Similarly, in fairly recent times, land averaged 15% of the cost of a new home. In most areas, it is now up to 40%.

Land continues to be a major path to big real estate profits.

HOW TO FIND AND PROFIT
FROM LITTLE-KNOWN LAND TRACT DEALS

You don't have to compete with foreign investors fleeing from their own countries with their funds to buy up their many thousands of American acres of farmland. You don't have to put up front the many millions of dollars our own big development corporations invest in land tracts. You just have to be in the right place at the right time. And you alone, in contrast to these foreign and corporate grants, possess the secret ingredients needed to find and make fortunes from these land tract deals! You are local. You are there. You know your area, its inhabitants, its tract owners, its local development laws and its road and other growth patterns. All you have to do is channel and focus this *local* knowledge and experience, along with not too many investment dollars, to make big profits from land tract deals.

How I Made Big Profits in Land Without Any Risks

For instance, you can be a middleman in land tract sales. Some say "speculator." By any name, such informed local investment unearths little-known land tract deals for big profits. A few years ago, with two local partners, I bought 80 vacant acres of non-working farmland adjacent to a small village about 50 miles north of New York City. We found out through a mutual relative of the farmer and one of my partners that the farmer-owner was retiring and wanted to sell. We paid $2200 per acre for the 80 acres (or $167,000) and signed a contract-option with purchase terms as follows: $5000 non-refundable option payment on signing of contract, a total of 15% (including the $5000 option amount) down on closing, balance on purchase money mortgage held by seller, three years interest only (8%), then principal and interest for 12 years. In addition to the three-year, no principal clause to ease start-up development costs, there were other provisions to release land from the mortgage whenever needed for lot sales, subordination clauses to permit banks to lend money for construction on the land as first mortgage ahead of this overall purchase money mortgage on the tract, and other similar builder-type contract clauses. The main option clause was that for our $5000 option money, we, as the buyers, were given 18 months with extension if needed, to get local preliminary subdivision approval under the local zoning ordinances, which permitted up to 2.5 detached houses and/or apartments per acre on a planned unit development basis. Sewers and water were available on a contract basis from the adjoining village.

Within 90 days of our signing the above contract-option, a local builder-developer bought it from us @ $3500 per acre and paid us $20,000 in cash then, non-refundable for the contract. Fifteen months later, he received his subdivision approval. A simultaneous closing was then held with us, the original farmer-ower and the builder. Our profit was $113,000, less the $5000 down payment and $2000 in legal fees.

THE FOUR STEPS TO SUCCESSFUL REAL ESTATE DEALING

As in all successful real estate deals, the technique employed here was a straightforward, step-by-step procedure which carefully touched all these bases:

Step 1. *Know and investigate the area.* Regional factors for residental development and localization are the keys to land value. Many localized factors affect each land tract, including "no- and slow-growth" zoning environmental concerns, coastal and wetland use controls, commuter distances to employment, regional and local economy. "Will homes sell in this area?" is really the basic question.

Step 2. Find the tract. Local knowledge and contacts are invaluable. There are just so many large tracts that have development potential in each area. Get to know every one. You're in the best local position to know first when one comes up for sale. Even if a tract you like is not for sale, you may be able, as a local person, to solicit its sale by offering above-market purchase price, *if* you get good working option and developer-type terms. One partner I worked with would offer land-owners "tomorrow's price today" to get them to sign up. It turned out that his "tomorrow's price," with inflation and built-in housing de-mand, turned out to be "yesterday's price" shortly after we purchased and structured the deal.

Step 3. Analyze the tract. Factors intrinsic to the tract such as its location, topography, appearance, views, subsurface conditions, drain-age and access are critically important when you are determining whether a tract is feasible for proposed residential land subdivision. Even if you do buy (as is strongly suggested here) on an option basis only, you don't want to throw away your time and option money. See Feasibility Study Field Checklist for Land Subdivisions in Figure 6-1. Remember, as with the area, the final practical question is "Will homes on this tract sell?"

Step 4. Negotiate the deal. If your feasibility check warrants it, negotiate the deal. You have either appraised the land or had it ap-praised on a market approach basis. As stated, you don't have to press for a bargain—*if* you get the option and developer terms you want. If you are just buying the land for profit from future land value increases, then negotiate at or below market price and be prepared to sweat it out over a period of time, maybe years, of taxes and payments, as foreign investors and big development corporations can and do. If you are a local investor, interested in finding little-known tract deals for com-paratively quick, enormous turnover profits, don't try to compete with these well-endowed giants. Pay the going per-acre rate (or even slightly more if you have to) and structure the deal on an *option*, developer-type basis. And hire a lawyer experienced with drawing the clauses typical to such tract deals.

HOW TO PROFIT FROM LITTLE-KNOWN
PUBLIC WATER, SEWER AND OTHER CHANGES

Roads, public sewers, public water and zoning are the "four horsemen" that spur land profits. In the 19th century, population centers, eventually cities, followed wherever railroad tracks were laid in our country. After WWII, our suburbs grew by expansion from cities along existing and new road networks like the interstate high-way system. Now another suburban development pattern has been added—the public utility pattern.

FEASIBILITY FIELD CHECKLIST
FOR RESIDENTIAL LAND SUBDIVISIONS

LOCATION _____

OWNER _____DATE _____

THE COMMUNITY	MILES
1. Schools	
2. Jobs	
3. Local shopping	
4. Major shopping	
5. Parks	
6. Churches	
7. Hospitals	
8. Nearest development	
9. Master plan	

THE LAND	YES	NO
11. Accessible		
12. Adverse views		
13. Adverse traffic		
14. Smoke, fumes		
15. Flooding		
16. Landslide		
17. Subsidence		

THE LAND (cont'd.)	YES	NO
18. Air traffic		
19. Existing fill		
20. Acceptable topo		
21. Needs fill?		

THE UTILITIES	YES	NO
22. Public water		
23. Fire protection		
24. Electric		
25. Phone		
26. Street lighting		
27. Garbage removal		
28. Police protection		
29. Storm sewers		
30. Paved street		
31. Public transport		
32. Zoning		
33. Growth area?		
34. Master plan?		

35. List 3 comparable land tracts and lot prices assigned to each:

_____ $_____

_____ $_____

_____ $_____

36. Air quality _____ 37. Water quality _____

38. Environmentally OK? _____

39. Typical lot size in area _____

40. Typical lot price $_____ 41. Suitable for development _____

42. REMARKS (key to above nos.)_____

_____

_____

_____

_____

_____

_____

FIGURE 6-1: Feasibility Field Checklist for
Residential Land Subdivision

Development of our homes, shopping centers and industrial parks in recent years has become feasible only wherever public utilities, sewer and water exist or are proposed. For many years after WWII, suburban development took place using individual systems like septic tanks and wells. Private commercial systems also were used wherever soils and well yields were favorable—and often where they were not. Recently, because of environmental and community slow-growth concerns, development in most areas is being limited more and more to public utility locations.

Whenever main roads are given new interchanges or new routes are proposed, land values boom. I have seen and profited from startling increases in commercial land parcels alongside new road interchanges—often from as little as $500-an-acre farmland to as much as $150,000 for one acre abutting the interchange!

A zoning change permitting mobile homes under certain conditions recently quadrupled the value of one large tract the day the mobile home amendment was enacted in my town.

Here is a step-by-step procedure for locating areas where proposed public water, sewer and road zoning changes will also change value and create little-known, local profit opportunities.

CHECKLIST OF PROCEDURES FOR LOCATING LITTLE-KNOWN, LOCAL, LAND PROFIT OPPORTUNITIES

ZONING

Step 1. See your town clerk. Get a copy of the zoning ordinances, all change sheets and a copy of the zoning map. Study these documents carefully. You will find many zoning situations, often little known to the people who inhabit such zoned districts.

Step 2. Arrange to get all future zoning changes. If you can get on the town clerk's mailing list for changes, fine. If not, drop by occasionally. Changes may mean profits.

Step 3. Read legal notices on zoning changes. Local papers publish these required legal notices. Read them regularly.

ROADS

Step 1. Get to know the state highway engineer. Find out at the highway office what roads or interchanges are planned in your region. Follow up regularly.

Step 2. Contact the County Highway Dept. as in Step 1.

PUBLIC SEWER, WATER—(This is now probably the most important development factor.)

Step 1. Locate all proposed sewer districts in your region. This is where the action will be. In practically all areas it is no longer feasible for developers to build their own commercial sewer and water plants. It takes too many years to get approval and it costs too much. Public sewer and water is now the name of the game—and federal funds are subsidizing communities to build and extend public sewers and water systems to improve the environment.

HOW TO ANNEX FOR PUBLIC UTILITIES
AND PROFITS

Our land consists of tens of thousands of political municipalities. There are cities, villages, towns, boroughs, counties, each with its own local government and its own public network of roads and utilities. During the past three decades, much of our land development of houses, services and people spread from the cities into the towns, which often did not have adequate public water and sewers. As need for adequate water and pollution of water increased because of these "spread cities" built with individual wells, septic sewer systems and other inadequate private and community utilities, government environmental controls also increased. The federal government through its Environmental Protection Agency and other agencies now encourages and subsidizes building of municipal water and sewer plants. Local planning boards in many locations discourage building with private utilities.

There is a little-known, highly profitable way to cash in on this current development. Most towns which do not have public utilities adjoin or surround geographically the more densely populated cities and villages which do have or are getting adequate water and sewer systems. If you can locate a property which is in the town abutting a city or village and get it annexed politically to the city or village, you will increase its value many times over. A step-by-step procedure for annexation goes as follows:

BLUEPRINT FOR LAND ANNEXATION PROFITS

First Step. Study a tax map of the town that shows property lines as well as municipal boundary lines.

Second Step. Locate a property which does adjoin the village or city line that is for sale or that can be solicited for purchase.

Third Step. Make an offer at current market value for the property. Make it an option offer subject to your filing for and getting approval for annexation of the property to the village or city.

Fourth Step. Apply for annexation to the village or city. Villages or cities generally encourage annexation to increase their ratables tax base; towns usually don't want to give up their property for the same reason. This legal process takes time. However, many applications for annexation are approved and profits are great. A 20-acre parcel I appraised immediately after annexation to the Village of _____, N.Y. had sewer and water and denser zoning available to it after annexation. It was resold for approximately ten times its original option cost to the purchaser when he had bought it while it was still in the town. There are similar parcels similarly situated along community boundary lines throughout our land.

OTHER SPECIAL HIGH-PROFIT, LITTLE-KNOWN REAL ESTATE DEALS

Real estate is dynamic and ever changing. The prior annexation technique is just one illustration of such special profit potential situations which involve special methods of figuratively "moving" developable land from one political jurisdiction to another. Real estate investing also has many other off-beat, special, local profit opportunities. Here are some more examples of off-beat deals and profitable techniques which can be investigated and followed up for big profits in your own area:

Case Histories of Little-Known Land Profit Techniques

1. *Abandoned Rights-of-Way.* A landowner I know in _____, N.Y. bought a 50-foot wide strip of land about two miles long, an abandoned railroad right-of-way, from the receiver of the defunct railroad. He paid $200 an acre or about $23,000 for the 11+ acres involved. He has since traded parts of the land to adjoining property owners who needed these parts to make their properties whole because the R.O.W. had bisected their land. He also traded part of his R.O.W. to another adjoining landowner for a sand and gravel bank which was what he really wanted in the first place. (The owner of the R.O.W. is in the aggregates business.) He then sold the balance of the land to adjoining property owners who wanted to extend their land. After three years of this real estate horse-trading, he has traded and sold off the whole R.O.W. He still owns the sand and gravel bank with about one million yards still to process and he has his $23,000 investment back in pocket—with a $10,000 cash profit to boot. This was an imaginative conversion and subdivision of an abandoned R.O.W. (See Chapter 14 for address to write to for railroad R.O.W. information.)

2. *Lakeside Gores.* In real estate parlance, a "gore" is not a bull fighter being pushed around by a bull. It is defined legally as a piece of land, generally small, irregular, odd-shaped, triangular or tapering. Often these gores were created by roads or railroads or utilities which cut off small pieces of property from their original parcels. No matter how they evolved, there are countless such gores of land everywhere, often practically valueless because they are too small to allow building of conventional buildings on them.

Yet their very defects become their special offbeat value when a knowledgeable local investor locates gores that border lakes or other bodies of water. "Riparian," another good real estate word, means pertaining to the bank of a river, a lake or a tidewater. The combined definition of "gore" and "riparian" adds up to more than either one alone. . . increased value. If you own or can locate a small gore of land that is riparian to, say, a lake, you can launch a boat and use the *whole* lake for recreation from your tiny gore . . . or the buyer you resell the gore to, at a big profit, can row or sail to his heart's content.

For example, in an area I know, a land well known as the Lake Region, there are literally hundreds of such small dots of land surrounding many of the lakes because roads run close to the lake edges. Ownership can be easily traced by going through assessors' maps and records. There is a big market for such land which has access to water. In this off-beat investment opportunity, it's not a question of whose proverbial ox is being gored, it's a matter of who gets to the lakeside gore first for riparian rights and profits.

HOW TO MAKE BIG MONEY FROM SCATTERED-LOT INVESTMENT

The Interstate Land Sales Act is a law that requires a seller of unimproved lots to give full disclosure. It was enacted to try to control the activities of many land companies that use high-pressure sales tactics to sell lots that are rarely improved with promised roads and utilities (Booklet HUD 357-1(5), Housing Urban Development (HUD), Washington, D.C.). Exempt from this law are developments where less than 50 lots are involved or where all lots are over five acres.

The key to big money from lot deals is not such boiler-room sales of inferior, underwater or desert land on *unimproved* "paper" roads from unsuspecting buyers. It is, instead, simply a matter of buying up scattered lots on *existing improved*, paved roads and reselling or subdividing them for resale. The procedure is simple, the technique methodical:

• *Drive throughout your area.* With street map in hand, check out all the existing town roads.

- *Stay off the private roads.* They are probably not maintained and often are not buildable because building permits may not be issued on private roads in many communities.
- *Spot all vacant attractive lots.* Look for good settings, good views, popular neighborhoods, recreational areas, wooded, lake and other potentially valuable locations.
- *Go to assessor's office.* The assessor has tax maps and records where you can locate ownership of these scattered lots.
- *Negotiate, purchase, subdivide.* Do this wherever possible and where existing road frontage is adequate.
- *Resell to individuals* (or to builders in quantity) for profit.

HOW TO FIND LAND FOR MOBILE HOMES

Zoning is the magic word for mobile homes. Without local permission by zoning right or special exception, there can be no mobile home development. True, the land must also be well located and suitable, but zoning is first in importance.

Statistics on demand for mobile home sites are overwhelming. By the late seventies almost nine million Americans were living in five million mobile homes. The mobile homes industry, in good and bad real estate times, has managed to deliver in most recent years from 17% to 30% of the single housing units built in the United States. As many as 600,000 mobile units a year have been manufactured and sold.

The demand and supply of mobile homes is there. The sites are not. Although the "climate" of local attitudes towards mobile homes is improving, there still are many communities that think mobile homes are jungles and that they lower adjoining property values. These attitudes are changing as more modern mobile home parks, built to modern standards, appear. Also, conventional and government financing for mobile homes makes these parks more feasible.

This complex of changing attitudes and overwhelming demand makes for increasing value and big profits on land for mobile homes.

The same procedures outlined in a prior section of this chapter on locating and profiting from residential land tract subdivisions apply here. In addition to using proper negotiation and contractual techniques, it is most important that once you have located the land you structure the whole deal on an *option* basis, subject to all authority approvals for a mobile home park or lot(s).

The step-by-step procedure for locating and profiting from land for mobile homes is as follows:

GUIDELINES ON PROFITING FROM LAND FOR
MOBILE HOMES

Step 1. Check all zoning ordinances. In most land tract locations, you find your site first, then check the zoning. In the case of mobile homes, you first find the zoning ordinance that permits mobile homes at a minimum of five per acre, then you locate a tract that meets the ordinance conditions.

Step 2. Locate the land. Check all sites that appear to comply.

Step 3. Check specific location. A proposed park should be free from and not substantially contribute to adverse scenic or environmental conditions and be conducive for residential purposes to meet federal guidelines and renters' desires: Convenient to schools, shopping, transportation, arterial road, community facilities? Affected by unacceptable physical hazards such as subsidence, floods, noxious gases, traffic hazards or danger from fire or explosion?

Step 4. Is site suitable? Are topography, subsoil conditions, soil bearing, site drainage, conducive for mobile home layout? Are neighboring usages existing or zoned for residential or for conducive uses? Are there adverse commercial or industrial neighbors? Any deed restrictions and covenants that may affect mobile home layout?

Step 5. Negotiate an option-purchase.

Step 6. Submit for local and other approvals. Or sell to a developer who will make the submissions to local planning board, etc.

An Example of Spectacular Profits

Profits can be spectacular. In one area I know, acreage land prices were about $3,000 per acre. One tract received preliminary paper approval for six mobile home sites per acre. It still looked the same the day after approval. Topographically, it still had the same appearance; its only change was in price. As a tract for mobile homes, it was now worth $1,500 per site or $9,000 per acre for 40 acres—a simple arithmetic change of $240,000 profit.

HOW TO PROFIT FROM LAND ZONED FOR
CLUSTERING, PLANNED UNIT DEVELOPMENT
AND CONDOMINIUMS

The youthful population pattern and baby boom bulges giving this last quarter-century its distinctive way of life also contrast with a "graying" of America. During the next half-century the number of people over 65 will double to 52 million, or one out of every six people. By the late seventies, there were 1½ million people over 65 in nursing homes. More land for retirement developments is a good investment bet for the future. This will be needed not just in southern regions with milder climates but in all parts of the country as well. Many older people don't want to leave familiar regions, their friends and their children. Retirement communities that are established on a condominium basis have been successful in all regions if properly located and developed. This aging trend not only makes land for condominum retirement developments and mobile home parks increasingly profitable investments but has also enhanced profit possibilities for travel facilities like budget motels.

Again, the secret ingredient of big profits from such land tracts is *zoning*. These modern, sophisticated development techniques are finding their way into more and more zoning ordinances in an increasing number of communities. These techniques are not esoteric. They are very practical and are being utilized to make land development and shelter construction more feasible economically, more functional in usage and more able to cope with the ever-decreasing supply of well-located, buildable land.

First, we must define our terms (see also Chapter 16):

• *Clustering.* A cluster development is a modern concept that evolved to cope with vanishing open space and growing urban sprawl. It generally means putting the same number of attached or detached housing units that are permitted by the zoning laws on smaller lots. This results in surplus land which can then be left as open space or improved with recreational facilities.

• *Condominiums and cooperatives. Condominium* is a Latin word meaning joint ownership or control. In housing, it means individual ownership of, say, an apartment, with unrestricted right to disposal of one's unit in its multi-unit project. The land and all other parts of the project are held or owned in common with owners of the other apartments. In a *cooperative*, the "co-op" corporation owns *all* the property including the individual unit. The apartment dweller, the member of the cooperative, owns not his apartment but a membership stock certificate in the cooperative corporation. Simply, a cooperative owns everything, a condominium owns nothing.

• *Planned Unit Development.* A PUD differs from a "condo" or "co-op" in that PUD owners own the land on which their home is located and they belong to a Home Owners Association which holds (owns) the common open space lands and other recreational facilities of their project. PUD also allows mixtures of various types of zoning so that different varieties of housing, usually on a clustered basis, can be combined with commercial establishments, office buildings, shopping facilities and even industrial buildings.

The same discovery and profit technique procedures and principles previously set down for residential land subdivisions and mobile home park land tracts apply as well to land tracts zoned for clustering, condos, cooperatives and PUDs.

This always involves careful review of zoning ordinances, regular follow-up for zoning changes and detailed investigation of specific locations that are so zoned. In growth areas, big profits are made regularly from locating land tracts that have such zoning and that are well located in terms of road access, public utility availability and suitable topography.

7

How to Find the "Hot Corner" Locations of Commercial and Industrial Land

Here is where you will find all the little-known ways to locate local big-return commercial sites. There are case examples of the really spectacular profits you can make from commercial land. There are chapter sections on how to spot and profit from "hot corner" commercial real estate at highway interchanges and at road changes in our car-dominated suburban-exurban communities. There is a section on how to cash in on recreational land investment. You are also shown here how to find sites for fast-food locations. There is a section on how to buy these commercial sites at or below market and how to sell them for big profits. Location is repeatedly stressed and detailed throughout this chapter and in the final section summary as the major criterion for finding and making maxi-profits from these little-known, local commercial land deals.

A Case Example of High Profits from Commercial Land

"Ma" Breger ran a local roadside corner bar on a main road intersection in a small town of 20,000. She also owned 24 acres and 2200 feet of road frontage on the two roads in front of the bar. When she decided to retire she told her lawyer to sell it all as one piece. She wanted none of the headaches and delays of subdivision.

As a broker for the buyers I arranged the sale of the acreage quickly for the listed price of $8,000 per acre, $192,000 total. I helped the investors subdivide the acreage into four parcels, one for a future shopping center site of 20 acres and three other one-acre sites for free-standing bank and fast-food commercial sites. Approval of the subdivision took five months. Resale of the four parcels took three weeks. Our investors sold the shopping center site for $22,000 an acre or $440,000. The bank site yielded $110,000. A fast-food chain bought one of the acre sites for $120,000. A "convenience store" chain bought the other for $100,000. Sales totaled $880,000—for a gross profit of $688,000.

How a $2000-Option Netted $36,000 Profit!

With another investor I located a dwelling on a ¾-acre plot with 200 foot road frontage, 400 feet away from a proposed limited access interchange ramp in a rural hamlet. We found this site by reviewing the proposed highway maps at the local State Highway Department Engineer's Office. These maps show all properties near proposed ramps. We offered the owner of the property $40,000, which was about 50% more than the appraised market value of the property. He accepted the offer which also involved giving him $2,000 for a six-month option on the property subject to our receiving local approval for a commercial fast-food operation on the site. We resold the deal to a national fast-food chain for $80,000. Rezoning approval was received and there was a simultaneous closing five months after original option. We netted a profit of $36,000 after all legal expenses for our option cost of $2,000.

HOW TO PROFIT FROM THE VALUE IMPACT ON COMMERCIAL REAL ESTATE OF OUR CAR-ORIENTED LIFE STYLE

Our nation moves on car wheels. So do the really big profits in real estate "ride" on spotting those good commercial locations which are most affected in value by this traffic.

To find these little-known, extremely profitable commercial locations in your local area, the most important data source is probably the office of the State Highway Superintendent, Auto Traffic Count Section. States plan their road improvements and get federal road subsidies based on the average daily traffic count (ADTC) which most highway departments monitor regularly on all important roads.

These records are public and available to you when you are looking for and checking out commercial land locations.

There is a small but growing trend in many communities to encourage location of small commercial buildings near populated areas to service walk-in trade. However, the major need for most successful commercial locations is still for a high ADTC. In the final analysis, all other factors being acceptable for commercial improvements, the total number of passing cars with proper access to the site is what makes value in most commercial parcels. Most fast-food chains specify minimum ADTC count of 10,000 ADTC for their proposed site locations. Budget-type motels won't consider sites unless they have a minimum 15,000 ADTC. Even if there is, say, a built-up area of hundreds of homes and apartments surrounding the site, many of these potential customers who could walk to the site still seem to use their cars anyway. The following is a finder's guide for locating and checking out commercial sites:

COMMERCIAL LOT FEASIBILITY CHECKLIST

RESEARCH THE SITE

- *Get car count ADTC.*
- *Check out curb cut regulations.* For example, in many areas, you can't get a curb cut permit for a driveway within 300 feet of an interstate highway interchange. The best commercial location has no value if its potential customers are not allowed to drive into it.
- *Check out sign laws.* Most communities have maximum size, number, and location sign laws. If too restrictive, the site may not be functional or marketable because potential customers won't know what's on it as they flash by.
- *Review zoning law and map.* It's usually best to make sure that specific commercial usages are permitted by right. Don't bet your investment money that you can get a variance or an exception approval from the local planning board. Or if you have to do so, buy the land only on option subject to getting such approval.
- *Check out utilities.* If public sewer and water are not available, does land have adequate percolation for septic system sewage disposal and water yield from wells? This can be very important. Commercial usages like laundries and restaurants and fast-food sites put heavy demand on utilities. Private facilities may seriously restrict potential commercial tenants and the site's value.

INSPECT THE SITE

- *Walk the site.* Note particularly whether the size, shape and topography of the plot are conducive for commercial improvements.

• *Is major cut and/or fill required?* The best-located site may be unfeasible if a mountain of rock has to be moved.
• *Is drainage pattern positive?* Does water drain off lot?

INSPECT THE BLOCK AND VICINITY

• *Drive past the plot.* In the vicinity, check particularly whether buildings (and signs) erected on the plot would have good visibility from both directions.
• *Note all neighboring uses.* Check particularly for similar proposed commercial uses that are already existing and that may make this site unfeasible. Check also for nearby unsightly, odorous or other adverse uses that may decrease the site's commercial appeal and value.

FIND MARKET VALUE

• *Secure comparable lot sales data.* See Chapters 5 and 7 for sources and techniques on how to find what the parcel is worth in the current market.
• *Check out the comparable properties.* Look at all the comparable recent land sales you unearthed and compare them to the property you are analyzing. Come to your studied opinion of market value.

HOW TO MEASURE GOOD CAR ACCESS, PARKING AND TRAFFIC COUNT

You have to know how to get accurate traffic counts. The following step-by-step procedure should be done for each commercial site.

Step 1. Contact the appropriate Auto Traffic Count Section. Their official auto traffic count booklets give car count locations by road name, number of cars, intersections and dates on which counts were taken. Each count is for average daily car traffic.

Step 2. Proportion the ADTC if necessary. If the ADTC booklet shows, say, 15,000 ADTC per day at the nearest major intersection, relate this 15,000 count to your site. Do all the 15,000 cars go by your site or do some turn off beforehand? You may have to proportion the count by estimating or by actual personal count.

Step 3. Relate the data to the site. For example, is this site for a motel which gets most of its business from overnight guests? Do most of the 15,000 cars whiz by during the day or does a good proportion pass in late afternoon and evenings? If the highway agency does not have hourly car counts available, you may have to go out again, click-counter in hand, to approximate such needed traffic flow.

• Does a curve, overgrown trees on another's property or hilly road obscure the property until too late to brake safely and turn into the plot?

- Are there acceleration and deceleration lanes or shoulders?
- Does the road in front of the property have a middle island that cannot be crossed?
- Do cars on the opposite side therefore have to go too far to expect them to U-turn?
- Is the ADTC therefore cut in half?

Step 4. Check on parking facilities. Adequate room and gradient for parking for commercial sites is of paramount importance. If you have a top site and plenty of traffic but no room to put the cars of all the customers, what good is the site? Just for example . . . professional office buildings require four square feet of parking for every square foot of building, neighborhood food centers specify maximum 4% grades so that shopping carts in lot won't roll off lot and into cars, most shopping centers won't sign leases unless there is a 1 to 3.5 parking ration. Thus, if the store is 40,000 square feet or about one acre, 3½ acres of parking are needed.

HOW TO GET HIGH RETURNS FROM RECREATIONAL LAND

The booming leisure-recreation industry is setting new records. Even though this is a trendy, faddish business, with millions of people switching from bowling to skiing to tennis to racquetball, the overall leisure-recreation industry graph line is constantly up. An affluent middle class and a vast generation of post WWII "babies" now bulging population charts with their outdoor sports-oriented life styles appear to assure continued overall growth to this industry.

Land for recreation is in great demand: a piece of land on a lake or with lake rights to get on the lake, a small tract of a few acres on or near a good fishing stream, a few acres of woodland in the hills or some open space with good views. As our country becomes more urbanized, suburbanized and exurbanized, millions yearn for and look to locate on such land parcels not too far from where they live and work. It can be used just for regular outings, for a day's fishing, hunting or camping, for a second home or for current or eventual retirement. Recent government statistics show that one out of every 12 Americans owns either a vacant lot or second home and the percentage is still growing. This revealing information highlights the current hunger for land, good recreational land particularly.

For instance, there was no art to getting rich on recreational land in Atlantic City in New Jersey once it became a legal gambling mecca. It's just that the local property owners and investors were there when the lightning struck and fortunes were made in land for casinos and allied commercial usages. The same thing applies locally anywhere in our land where land for recreation is available. The key is *being there, being local, knowing the area.* Do you hunt, fish, camp? Are you familiar with woodland open space or lake lands in your local area or within a three- to four-hour drive of your urban-suburban area?

How One Fisherman Reeled In "10-Times" Profits

A local merchant I know spent the last ten years running his store in town and hunting and fishing on his days off in hills about two to three hours away. During these years, he got to know many of the people in the area he hunted. He was offered land and bought it, much of it at prices below $200 an acre. This local merchant still runs his store and still hunts and fishes on his days off. He has also been selling off pieces of this recreational mountain land he owns. Only now, the price per acre is about $2,000, ten times what he paid. He has made a living from his store in town. He has made a fortune from his local knowledge and investment in land where he hunts and fishes.

The techniques for scattered lot investment detailed in Chapter 6 and in minor subdivisions in Chapter 8 are equally applicable to recreational land investment. As in those other land dealings, the main thread in all such successful land investment is being there first, being local, knowing the area.

HOW TO MAKE BIG PROFITS AT HIGHWAY INTERCHANGES AND ROAD CHANGES

When the major sections of the interstate highway system were being built during the sixties and seventies, gas companies bought up thousands of sites adjoining the highway interchanges for high-gallonage gas stations. The prices of such sites, generally an acre or less, was about $200 an acre for the many rural locations involved to as much as $200,000 for the same acre as soon as the highway interchange location was known . . . a startling example of the rise in value for commercial sites wherever there is strong, competitive demand.

I bought, sold and appraised many of these sites in four states during this period and learned many things about them, some the hard way:

• Since these highways were built with federal 90% subsidy, the states that built them had to adhere to federal road specifications.

• One of these specifications required the states to permit no curb cuts for driveway entrances on the intersecting minor road for a distance of 300 feet from the on-off ramp to the interstate highway.

• This one requirement immediately made the particular property that started or had access beginning 301 feet from the ramp the first and foremost parcel for value, the one everyone wanted, the 200,000 "best shot" site. This was the first property to get the cars coming off for gasoline, for dinner, for a motel.

• The property closest to the ramp, within the 300-foot restriction, was generally bypassed. In many rural areas, it's still only worth not much more than the original $200 an acre.

A LITTLE-KNOWN WAY
TO LOCATE HIGH-PROFIT COMMERCIAL SITES

Now that this interstate system is largely complete, most of these bypassed parcels adjacent to the ramps are still available at low prices because of this restriction. For example, a budget motel depends for its traffic mainly on transients and needs sites with good visibility but cannot pay top land prices because of the budget motels' construction cost limitations. These low-cost sites adjacent to ramps are ideal for such use *if* an easement or right-of-way can also be purchased through property that is more than 300 feet from the ramp. The key to development and profits from such bypassed commercial site locations is purchasing an option, subject to getting such R.O.W. access and subject to getting proper commercial zoning for the contemplated use.

This is only an example of the basic search-and-find procedure for unearthing little-known, local, very high-profit commercial sites. It applies also to road changes other than highway interchanges. The same systematic procedures laid down in earlier sections of this chapter and in Chapter 8 apply here also. America is in love with its cars and is constantly changing and improving the roads that service its car-oriented way of life. Roads are being planned and changed everywhere all the time. Road changes also create and increase commercial land values, often spectacularly. Strip commercial development in our suburban society is still where we mainly shop. Stay in contact with the state and local highway and planning offices. Know your area. You are there. Road changes are where the big profits abound.

HOW TO FIND THE HOT SITES FOR FAST-FOOD LOCATIONS

The same site selection criteria that governed the many thousands of gasoline service stations that were installed during recent decades on interstate and other highways now govern fast-food site selection. Fast-food sites are still being sought, found and built on in suburban, exurban, and urban locations.

These free-standing fast-food and convenience stores are now everywhere in our suburbs. Fast-food chains like MacDonalds and Burger King have expanded from our suburbs into storefront locations in our cities and even internationally. In the suburbs, land costs for such sites run from about $50,000 to $150,000 per site. However, the modern American phenomenon of eating out at fast-food restaurants is catered to not just by these franchised and wholly owned giants. It is also serviced by smaller group and individual retail stores.

Commercial real estate in the suburbs is dynamic. For example, thousands of neighborhood gas stations were made obsolete by the interstate highway system. Many such obsolete sites, because of good neighborhood commercial location, were then converted or rebuilt for neighborhood convenience or fast-food commercial use. Our suburban way of life has transformed our nation's eating and shopping habits.

NINE KEY FACTORS FOR FAST-FOOD LOCATIONS

- Adequate local population
- Visibility of site
- High traffic count
- Large visible sign permission
- Good access
- Adequate frontage
- Commercial use permitted by zoning
- Acceptable topography; level or can be made level enough economically for building and parking improvements
- Large enough for required number of car parking spaces.

HOW TO BUY AND SELL
COMMERCIAL SITES FOR BIG-TICKET PROFITS

Once you've found that local "hot-corner" commercial site, your first step is to buy it. Your final step is to sell it for profit. It's the steps you take in between purchase and resale as detailed in the following checklist that ensure maximum profit.

CHECKLIST OF PROCEDURES FOR COMMERCIAL
LOT SALES

• *Step 1. Appraise the property.* Hire a professional appraiser or appraise it yourself if you are knowledgeable about local commercial values, using market approach and analysis of recent similar comparable sales.

• *Step 2. Buy on option.* The best-located site can be valueless for commercial purposes if it can't get local approvals. You must purchase only on option subject to getting all necessary zoning, health, environmental, and any other local approvals needed for commercial locations.

• *Step 3. Tailor the purchase contract for easy resale.* If your site is right, the purchase price right and your option provisions right, then your eventual profits will be assured . . . if certain other critical purchase terms and conditions are made part of the original purchase contract:

(a) *Right to assign.* It is most important that this provision be put in the contract so you can assign or "sell" your contract to the eventual commercial site developer. Often these buyers want to do the site planning and get all the local approvals based on their own plans and specifications. Besides, it will often make simultaneous closings possible on both your contract to buy and your contract to resell. This can save you from laying out large sums to close your buying transaction and then waiting for another closing to make your profit. It also often makes it possible to make large profits based on your comparatively low option payment only.

(b) *Seller's agreement to cooperate in submissions.* Your contract must include a provision that the seller will agree to join as the landholder of record in all applications for local zoning and other approvals.

• *Step 4. Find the commercial buyer.* The whole thrust of this chapter is how to make big profits happen from commercial land deals. Once you have used these search, locate, option-buy techniques to package a hot-corner commercial site, buyers will beat a path to your door if you use the normal real estate sales channels. You still have to touch all the sales bases to get maximum sales exposure: list with all the brokers, particularly commercial brokers; advertise in the proper places; notify real estate offices of appropriate commercial chains; yes, even put a good for-sale sign on the property itself, since by definition, it will have a very good visible location with plenty of automobile and other commercial exposure.

A BLUEPRINT FOR COMMERCIAL LAND PROFITS

Location, location, location. . . . This ancient real estate adage is particularly true for commercial land value. There are many factors that make for residential value. Some people like to live on hilly heights so they overlook views and their neighbors below. Others like to be on or near lakes, golf courses, development lots near many neighbors, or on large plots, etc. Industry usually likes to locate where there are utilities and where level land and good transportation to markets are available.

In the case of commercial real estate, there is really only one basic question: Can you make money on that location; will the business that will tenant that land be successful? *Location* heads the commercial hot-corner checklist. Without a good location, all other factors like topography, drainage and even proper commercial zoning go for nought.

To summarize this modern approach to commercial land value:

    • *Our suburban-exurban way of life* has overriding impact on commercial lot value.

    • *Dynamic population movement*, region to region, city to suburb to exurb, makes for new "hot" commercial locations daily.

    • *Increased leisure time* of our expanding population is constantly creating new demands for well-located commercial sites for tennis clubs, commercial exercise centers and health spas, sporting goods supply centers, racquetclubs, etc.

    • *Good car access, car count and adequate parking* are now and foreseeably the major criteria that make for good commercial location.

    • *Local knowledge* of what's happening is the name of the big profit game in commercial land location. For example, if you know that a large residential or industrial development is being planned in your area, the nearby access roads almost invariably become the "hot" strip for commercial centers that will service these developments. Profits can be enormous from investment in land so located if done based on local knowledge and careful research.

8

How to Make Major Profits from Minor Subdivisions

We deal here with *minor subdivisions*, that real estate creative technique so little known and so profitable. This chapter starts with details on how you use your local knowledge to locate and subdivide small land parcels for residential, commercial or industrial lot resale and/or development. Then there are various sections on how to get into minor subdivisions . . . on the key factor of road frontage . . . on zoning . . . on the "less than five lots" yardstick . . . on how you file your maps legally for approval where there are no planning boards . . . on how to get quick subdivision approvals where there are planning boards . . . and finally, how to sell these lots for major profits after your minor subdivision plans are approved.

HOW TO LOCATE AND
SUBDIVIDE SMALL PARCELS

Like Chapter 6 on residential land development, this chapter zeroes in on profits from land subdivision. However, there is one major difference between large and minor subdivisions, and that is the amount of up-front investment money needed, not the amount of profits. Large subdivisions need large investments. On the other hand, profits can be very high, even spectacular, on minor subdivisions compared to the relatively low investment usually involved.

How $7,000 Earned $37,000

For example, one minor subdivision deal I was involved in started with an advertisement offering 5½ acres for $15,000. My investigation of this newspaper ad showed that the land had 325 feet of public road frontage on one road and 105 feet on another road. It was a "through" parcel with frontage on roads in back and in front of the parcel. The price appeared to be about 25% above the going market price for this location. However, it was a good marketable area with good to very good homes in the vicinity and good views from the property. The key factors of road frontage and zoning were favorable for subdivision into four lots, the usual legal maximum for minor subdivisions. (See Figure 8-1.) Although overpriced, the land was purchased anyhow. Subdivision approval was received in three months and the four lots sold in less than a year for an average price of $14,000 each. *Cost*—$15,000 plus $4,000 in engineering, other subdivision fees and carrying costs, totaling $19,000. Total out-of-pocket investment was only $7,000 because part of the purchase price was repaid from cash flow from lot sales. *Net profit*—$37,000 on a $7,000 investment returned in less than a year on this "overpriced" parcel converted into big profits through modern, minor subdivision techniques.

Double Your Money in Two Months

I recently appraised the current market value of two 30,000 ± sq. ft. lots just subdivided by another investor in a minor subdivision of a 1½-acre parcel on an existing town paved road. The investor was a local person, familiar with the area and its landowners. He had learned that the 1½ acres were for sale for $20,000. Even though this was above market price, he did not haggle. He bought it because he first read the local zoning code and knew two lots could be subdivided and meet the regulations regarding minimum size, side yards, setback and road frontage. It took two months and $1200 in engineering and legal fees to receive minor subdivision approval. I appraised the lots for $17,500 each and he sold them for $17,000 each immediately. Net profit on his $6500 of up-front cash investment— $12,500!

These deals both exhibit many of the critical elements necessary for successful minor subdivision. As in general land subdivision on larger tracts, you have to know your area, its economy and its neighborhoods. Many localized factors affect each land parcel includ-

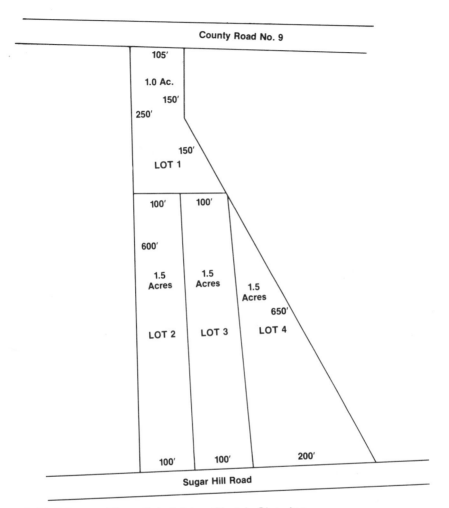

County Road No. 9

105'

1.0 Ac.

150'

250'

150'

LOT 1

100'   100'

600'

1.5 Acres   1.5 Acres   1.5 Acres

650'

LOT 2   LOT 3   LOT 4

100'   100'   200'

Sugar Hill Road

FIGURE 8-1: Minor Subdivision Sketch Showing
Property Subdivided into Four Lots

ing "no- and slow-growth" zoning and environmental concerns. Also, factors intrinsic to the tract itself are important, such as its location, topography, subsurface conditions, drainage and access. Where will the buyers work? If recreational plots are involved, is the property within a three-to-four hour drive from where buyers live and work? What are lots selling for in the area? Feasibility boils down to the final question—will the lots sell? These are the general feasibility questions.

Here are the specific minor subdivision tools you use to answer these questions and to locate, check out, subdivide and make big profits from such minor subdivisions:

• *Local zoning.* Check out particularly lot width or frontage requirements.

• *Road frontage.* The more frontage you have compared to total area, the better chance you have to make salable lots. Also make sure the parcel is on a *public* maintained road; some communities bar subdivision on private roads.

• *State subdivision laws.* Many states define "minor subdivision" as less than five lots. Most state laws permit local planning boards to give final approval to such "minor subdivisions" without additional state or county health department, environmental and other state agency approvals. This cuts down drastically subdivision processing time, often from years to months. Mortgage expense, engineering and submission costs are also far lower.

• *Planning board submissions.* You need a competent professional engineer or surveyor to make your submissions. You also need to know the subdivision requirements intimately before you make formal submissions. If you research these requirements with the local building inspector or town engineer first, you'll save time—which is money in subdivision work.

• *Option-purchases.* In all cases, your offer to purchase should be made on an option basis, subject to investigation, feasibility report and, if at all possible, also subject to at least preliminary minor subdivision approval.

• *Stress location.* As in scattered-lot location (Chapter 6) look for good settings, good views, popular neighborhoods, recreational areas, wooded lake and other potentially valuable residential or commercial locations. Use assessors' records to locate ownership of parcels you find that are suitable for minor subdivision.

HOW SMALL DEVELOPERS CAN MAKE BIG PROFITS

Large land developers, if successful, reap large subdivision profits based on very large investments and long lead times. Minor subdividers can do better proportionately with much less regulation. For instance, as detailed more fully in Chapter 6, the Federal Interstate Land Sales Act controls sellers of unimproved lots because many land companies have used "boiler-room" sales techniques to sell lots which are rarely improved with promised roads and utilities.

If you sell lots from a minor subdivision you are not so controlled. First, you have less than 50 lots which this Interstate Land

Sales Act does not control. Most important, you are offering lots on paved, public roads which you don't have to build because they were already there when you bought the parcel you later subdivided.

Quick $100,000 Profit

It is not just residential land that can be subdivided on a "minor" basis. Commercial land can also be so subdivided. For example, there is the real estate deal previously mentioned concerning the four-acre site @ $25,000 per acre which I had bought with several partners: Although a larger investment was involved, a quick minor subdivision (90 days) resulted in a $100,000 profit on a $10,000 down payment. Minor subdivisions can lead to big profits whether they be residential, commercial or industrial.

THE "MAGIC TRINITY"

Road frontage, zoning and less than five lots . . . these are the three important bases for successful minor subdivisions. Most areas label minor subdivisions "less than five lots." The beauty of this type of minor land subdivision work is that if you want to deal in many lot sales, you can still do so. Just keep each subdivision at less than five if so defined in your area. *The arithmetic is simple.* The lots don't necessarily have to be small lots. I've taken 20-acre tracts and broken them into four five-acre lots. People rushed to buy them for small farmettes. As long as you can retail all the subdivided pieces of the property pie for more than you paid for the whole, you're making profits. This is so because you are creating lots on *paper only*, legally, through subdivision, without having to put in expensive roads and utilities. In the case of the 20 acres that were bought for $1500 per acre, the subdivided four large five-acre lots were sold for $17,500 each. This simple arithmetic resulted in a $40,000 profit on this one deal. This is the major secret ingredient—*road frontage.* It's either there as an existing road when you buy the property or you don't buy.

The *amount* of road frontage of course can be variable, based on the kind of zoning involved. For instance, one zoning ordinance where I've subdivided on this basis defines *width of a lot* as "the mean dimension measured at substantially right angles to the depth of the lot." If you look at the sketch on page 99, you'll see that this definition was important because zoning required a minimum 100 foot lot width and irregular Lot 4 met this definition. This meant an additional $14,000 in lot sales for this one lot.

Other zoning ordinances define minimum lot widths by the

length of frontage at the road, some at a setback of 30 feet back from the road, etc. Careful review of zoning requirements, full investigation of possible properties and your own local knowledge of what is required and what is salable in the area, are what pay off. Still another illustration of variable requirements that make for big profits are those communities which permit "flag lots." The "Pikes Peak" subdivider used as an example in Chapter 1 was permitted under that Colorado zoning ordinance to do a minor subdivision of seven (not just the usual four lots) with six five-acre lots and one large 15-acre lot. He was able to do this because the zoning ordinance permitted this very large lot in the subdivision to be approved, even though it had only 50-foot wide access frontage on the public road. (See Figure 8-2.)

HOW TO FILE MAPS WHERE THERE ARE NO PLANNING BOARDS

In some less populated towns, there are no planning boards and no zoning ordinances. These areas often are excellent locations for residential subdivisions and for recreational second home lots or for

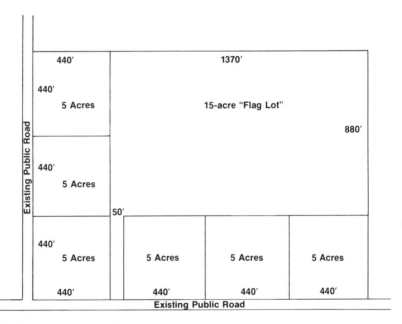

FIGURE 8-2: Sketch Showing 40 Acres
Subdivided into Seven Lots

commercial-service type lots at important highway interchanges, usually in rural areas. The fastest growing U.S. counties now are those with a population of no more than 2500!

The same prudent feasibility-research techniques must be used in such areas as in the more populated, sophisticated controlled areas. The Federal Interstate Land Sales Act provisions previously detailed still apply. You still have to make certain that the location chosen for subdivision has existing good roads and is one where lots will sell. You still have to hire competent professional engineers or surveyors, familiar locally, to lay out the subdivision, draw the maps and write the legal descriptions. The difference is mainly in terms of time. Such subdivisions can be processed to final approval very quickly. There is no planning board to submit the subdivision plan to for approval. In some areas, the local town board signs the map. Often, when the map is finished, all you have to do is take it to the local deeds records office, most of the time to the County Clerk's office, and get the map recorded. It then becomes a legally filed map and you can sell or build the subdivided lots.

HOW TO GET QUICK PLANNING BOARD APPROVALS

As our nation has become more and more suburbanized, most formerly rural communities have learned, often from sad experience with developers, to control their growth. Federal subsidies have encouraged community planning and paid for the drawing up of community master plans, county tax maps and model zoning ordinances. Along with such professional growth controls also come local reaction to formerly uncontrolled growth. In many local areas, even in some whole states and regions, there are definite no- and slow-growth patterns of controls in operation. Large-lot zoning and banning or limiting of apartment/town-house developments are one form. Also, strict area growth controls like the Ramapo Plan which began in Rockland County, N.Y., have spread to many other communities. This plan limits growth to denser portions of suburban areas that are already serviced by existing utilities and facilities.

The technique of minor subdivision is ideally adapted to this modern evolving no- and slow-growth pattern of suburban controls now prevalent almost everywhere. Most communities and their planning boards are concerned primarily with the large developments that bring in new hordes of people and require new services, utilities and facilities. Small, local, minor subdivisions using existing roads and facilities usually are not fought against or delayed officially or by neighbors' reactions; they are often encouraged, particularly if they are larger lots. You can expedite your planning board final approval by following this step-by-step procedure:

    • *Do complete feasibility.* Prepare your submission thoroughly. Do your homework completely. Know the zoning requirement intimately. Hire good local surveyors or engineers experienced in minor subdivision work.

    • *Contact local officials.* You can expedite your approvals and avoid "surprises" during formal submissions. You do this by sitting down informally with the building inspector, the town engineer and the planning board chairman when they are available, to discuss your submission and their requirements in advance of your formal submission. This also applies to other agencies like the county or state highway department if state or county highways are involved and if their agencies control approvals for driveway permits.

    • *Contact neighbors.* Most subdivision ordinances require you to legally notify by registered mail all property owners within a prescribed distance of the property you plan to subdivide. Often, a preliminary visit or contact and explanation of your plans, particularly with the immediate neighbors, will allay normal concerns and may avoid later formal objection to your subdivision. Planning boards are sensitive to community reaction.

    • *Make a complete submission.* Don't piddle about with your plans. Check and double-check all subdivision requirements. Make certain your engineer or surveyor has prepared *all* the required plans and data. Dot every "i" and cross every "t" required by the ordinance. I've often heard people say, "You have to give the board something to correct." This is simply not good policy. Turn in a sloppy, incomplete submission and you'll get nothing but delay, maybe outright rejection. There's big money to be made in minor subdivisions. The way to do it is the right way—the complete way.

HOW TO SELL
THESE MINOR SUBDIVISION LOTS

These quick, major profits will be yours if you apply your local knowledge and the guidance given here to this little-known real estate technique of minor subdivision. This whole book is on how to make real estate profits happen. Minor subdivisions are most creative profit-making happenings. You don't just stand there, waiting for profit lightning to strike. In minor subdivision, you make little pieces of land out of bigger pieces that have existing paved road frontage and permissive zoning. The building lots that result are the end product and *each* building lot has become a salable entity because of your efforts.

Sometimes a builder will buy the whole four-lot minor subdivision package from you on a wholesale price basis. In most cases, though, each lot will be sold separately on a retail, higher-price basis to individual builders and other lot buyers through normal sales outlets. These include real estate brokers, your signs on the lots themselves and newspaper advertising.

A buildable lot in our suburbanized-exurbanized country is a thing of value practically everywhere. You make this value and your profits happen when you create lots in minor subdivisions.

9

How to Find Little-Known Commercial and Industrial Opportunities

This chapter shows you how to locate commercial and industrial properties for investment and profit. Various evolving and new profit opportunities in our ever-changing suburban-urban land are detailed. There is a section on how to get into "budget" motel real estate deals. High-profit techniques are spelled out for converting obsolete gas stations on good, local, neighborhood commercial sites to new profitable modern uses. You're shown how to make high returns from small neighborhood shopping centers. There is a section on how to spot and profit from recreational-commercial investments. There are also sections on how to profit from regional growth and decline cycles . . . how to make big profits from industrial buildings with universal tenant appeal . . . how to use construction cost techniques to check out industrial buildings . . . and how to cash in on the boom in suburban professional office buildings.

HOW TO GET INTO BUDGET MOTELS

History repeats itself. In the thirties, travelers stayed overnight in roadside cabins. Then after WWII, they had to rent rooms in increasingly expensive "posh" motels luxuriously equipped with pools and other costly amenities they usually had no time to use. Now budget motels, without frills, are the fast-growing motel chain answer to a suburban-urban America always on the move . . . and an ever-increasing local profit opportunity.

The old pre-war "Mom and Pop" rural small motel for travelers has been made extinct by the 100+-unit motel, usually located near interstate and other major highway interchanges. There are various types of modern motels. In-city motor-hotels are usually in excess of 250 rooms. In resort areas, similar large motor-hotels offer resort and hotel services to vacationers. In the suburbs and along rural highway interchanges, the typical modern 100+-unit motel services businessmen and family travelers. The thrust here is on locating and profiting from such suburban roadside motels, particularly that comparatively recent phenomenon, the budget motel.

The budget motel evolved naturally as an answer to the needs of the businessman and touring motorist. Inflation and increasing room demand have brought average room rates to a $30-a-night average in standard motels like Howard Johnson, Holiday Inn, Ramada Inn, as well as in many independent, modern motels that offer pools, restaurants and other amenities. Although often underused, these amenities have to be reflected in room rentals. So budget motel chains like Super 8 Motels and Days Inns rose to meet this growing demand for reasonable, modern, well-kept motel rooms for overnight stay at recent average daily rates of $20. They usually have no pools and are located near restaurants.

A Case History of Budget Motel Land Profits

A land investor, Max D., located a seven-acre site on a busy arterial highway in a suburban area near a Midwest city. It had more than an 18000 average daily traffic car count (ADTC), and it was zoned for commercial use including motels and restaurants. The price asked was $150,000, all cash. Max contacted the real estate departments of several budget motel chains (see Figure 9-1). The site met the criteria of one chain which was actively looking to expand in the East.

He negotiated with the land owner and took an option for eight months on the property. The option cost was $7500 nonreturnable but applicable to the purchase price if he exercised the option.

The policy of this chain was to be near a restaurant but not to run one. So they referred him to another real estate department. This referral was to a national chain "pancake"-type restaurant which was often near their motels.

He made a deal with both chains. The motel would take four

acres, the restaurant 1½ acres and he would retain 1½ acres. The deal was subject to getting approval for this commercial minor subdivision and for motel and restaurant approvals.

A month before the option expired he received the subdivision and building permit approvals. He exercised the option, and had simultaneous closings with the original land owner and the motel and restaurant chains. Bottom profit line—his $7500 option cash investment plus $5500 in engineering and legal fees resulted in a $94,500 net profit in seven months (original cost—$150,000 plus $5,500 fees = $155,500 subtracted from a total of $250,000 paid him by the budget motel and restaurant chains for their two sites). In addition to the $94,500 profit, he still owned a 1½-acre commercial site made even more valuable by the motel-restaurant complex!

Figure 9-1 shows a list of the more important franchise and wholly-owned budget motel chains. Some buy or lease motel sites; others offer franchises to build and operate such motels. You can also get a National Directory of Budget Motels from Pilot Books, 347 5th Ave., New York, N.Y. 10016.

A LIST OF MOTEL CHAINS

American Family Lodge Denver, Colorado	Passport Inns of America, Inc. Memphis, Tennessee
Budget Inns Beverly Hills, Calif.	Red Roof Inns, Inc. Columbus, Ohio
Chalet Susse International, Inc. Nashua, New Hampshire	Regal 8 Inns Mount Vernon, Illinois
Days Inn of America Atlanta, Georgia	Roadrunner Motor Inns Houston, Texas
Econo-Travel Motor Hotels Norfolk, Virginia	Scottish Inns of America Kingston, Tennessee
Family Inns of America Rocky Mount, North Carolina	Spirit of '76 Inns Columbus, Ohio
Jolly-Ho Inns Daytona Beach, Florida	Thrifty Dutchman Coral Gables, Florida
Kampgrounds of America, Inc. Billings, Montana	Time-out Inns Ft. Lauderdale, Florida
Motel 6 Santa Barbara, Calif.	

FIGURE 9-1: A List of Motel Chains

In this very competitive yet high-profit motel business, budget motels appear to offer the best modern answer for profit returns from providing accommodations for travelers. Whether you want to sell or lease a motel site to such a chain or get in as a franchise owner-operator, you check out the deal the same way, using the following step-by-step procedure:

KEY STEPS TO MOTEL PROFITS

Step 1. Analyze location. For proposed sites or for purchase of existing budget motels, location is most important. Is there good visibility? Access from an interstate highway or major road? Is there a minimum 40,000 population in the vicinity? Near a large hospital? Near a university with a large student body? Other back-up locational influences?

Step 2. Review budget motel factors. What is the traffic count? (See Chapter 9.) How does it flow? Peak hourly counts? Easy access for major roads without complicated directional signs? Is there a restaurant nearby? Does the site have at least 150 feet of frontage (250 feet if an affiliated restaurant is also to be built)? For a successful modern motel operation, will it be tied into a computer for efficient reservations? Where and how far away is the competition?

Step 3. Analyze the zoning, other controls. Budget motels require as many as 60 units per acre. How many units are permitted? Do maximum size or height sign requirements restrict visibility? Any road changes contemplated? Is motel use by zoning right or by exception? Do building regulations permit prefabricated construction? (Some chains use prefab.)

Step 4. Analyze the site. Are topography, size, dimensions of site acceptable? Enough well yield, if no public water? Any adverse neighbors, smoke, odors, noise, undesirable views? Is there a steep highway grade in front of motel with revving truck engines at night?

Step 5. Analyze the proposed or existing building improvement. Does plan or building show safe, sanitary, durable construction? Exterior and interior materials need minimum maintenance? Design of halls, exits, stairs, windows per national and local fire safety standards? If a chain type motel is involved, are room design and layout similar? (Some travelers frequent same chains because they feel comfortable in familiar surroundings.)

Step 6. Analyze income-expenses. This is a special use business which is subject to many factors—occupancy rates in region, in area, in this motel, if existing. Is trend up or down? Supplies, labor, management, advertising, insurance, utilities, taxes, maintenance expenses—

analyze all these basic profit-loss items carefully for proposed or existing budget motels. The demand for reasonable, modern, no-frills rooms is good. Just check out feasibility of each deal carefully.

HOW TO CONVERT OBSOLETE GAS STATIONS TO MODERN PROFITABLE USES

There's nothing quite so dynamic in real estate as commercial property usage, values and profits, particularly in our suburbs. For example, many neighborhood gas stations were made obsolete by the Federal Interstate Highway system. Also, oil companies changed their policy to one of building and owning mainly high-gallonage stations on these busy new road interchanges rather than selling to neighborhood independent gas station dealers. Skyrocketing gas prices and profit ceilings have also made many independent stations unprofitable and obsolete. Many of these obsolete neighborhood stations were sold off or are available for conversion to other uses.

In most areas, because of good local, commercial neighborhood location, these gas stations with pumps removed or left in for self-service became, or can become, convenience, fast-shop or fast-food stores.

Examples of Gas Station Conversions

One enterprising dairy firm in southeastern New York recently bought up 50 old neighborhood gas stations, converted them into highly profitable, free-standing convenience stores and even sold (self-service) gas on some of the sites. Other successful uses, converted and foreseeable, are pizza stores, hamburger franchise, doughnut store locations and other retail commercial outlets.

The demise of the neighborhood gas station gives life to other profitable uses on these tens of thousands of "obsolete sites" in our suburban neighborhoods because our same modern suburban way of life has transformed our eating and shopping habits.

To determine whether a site is feasible for conversion, a step-by-step feasibility procedure, similar to the one used for the budget motel, should be used to check out the area, the location, the zoning, the building and the profit potential. In these types of conversion from one commercial use to another, it is most important to consider also the tax advantages inherent in such commercial conversions offered by recent tax legislation. (See Chapter 4.)

HOW TO PROFIT FROM
NEIGHBORHOOD SHOPPING CENTERS

There is a growing phenomenon in the shopping center industry. More and more regional and area large shopping centers are experiencing economic problems depending on location. Yet neighborhood shopping centers are experiencing continued profits. Builders and developers are again seeking small local sites that have good exposure to traffic and also have that all-important local back-up demand in the immediate vicinity. There are other benefits to the developer:

EVALUATING SMALL SHOPPING CENTERS
FOR LARGE PROFITS

- *Anchor stores* are not needed in neighborhood shopping centers. A Sears store or other giant store that has to be offered at very low unprofitable rentals is not needed in order to attract the much higher, more profitable rentals from satellite small stores in the large shopping centers.
- *Huge risk capital investments* are not necessary in neighborhood shopping centers.
- *Large, expensive land tract assemblies* are not needed.
- *Weak, economic areas* affect regional shopping centers much more than small neighborhood centers which mainly sell basic necessities and services.
- *Local knowledge* of busy, built-up or proposed neighborhoods pays off particularly well in such investment in neighborhood shopping centers.

An Example of Neighborhood Center Profits

Three formerly very successful tract homebuilder partners I know were driven recently into Chapter 11 bankruptcy by a combination of reduced demand in their economically depressed Northeast area location and by excessively high financing and construction costs. The only successful, thriving asset left from the economic wreckage of their homebuilding business was the neighborhood shopping center they had built in one small town where they last operated. This was a small center on two acres of land with only about 21,000 square feet in a one-story 200' × 70' building and 2000 square feet in another detached bank building. This small center with 15 specialty retail shops and bank is located on the main road so it draws traffic from this small town and a large surrounding area. It is also in the midst of hundreds of homes they had built, which also produce walk-in and drive-in customers. So, this small neighborhood shopping center, built almost as an afterthought while these builders were mainly building tract homes, survived the local depressed economic conditions and is still spinning off profits.

The 20,000 to 70,000 square foot neighborhood shopping center with or without a food supermarket should be analyzed as follows, whether it be for a proposed location or to buy an existing one:

HOW TO ANALYZE
NEIGHBORHOOD SHOPPING CENTERS

• *Investigate the trading area.* Where do the shoppers come from? Check population growth or decline, road network and any changes, employment, competition. A neighborhood center needs about 2500 households if it has a 20,000 to 50,000 chain food mart and about 20 retail small stores; less if there is no supermarket.

• *Check out car count, access, site visibility and parking.* This is vital for neighborhood shopping centers. Regional centers have their own drawing power because of their size; neighborhood centers need good location. (See Chapter 7 on how to measure good car access, parking and traffic count.) Most neighborhood centers need a 1-to-3½ parking ratio; i.e., for every square foot of building 3½ square feet of parking should be available.

• *Analyze the site.* Whether proposed or existing, it should be carefully field checked, analyzed for location, zoning, utilities, topography, competition and taxes.

• *Check it out for modern construction specifications.* This generally involves open span interiors, well lighted and air conditioned, with resilient floors. Beware of close column spacing, immovable partitions, poor delivery access and inadequate parking at improper, excessively high gradients.

HOW TO MAKE MONEY SAFELY
FROM RECREATIONAL COMMERCIAL
PROPERTIES

Leisure is one of America's biggest industries. Surveys indicate as much as $75 billion a year is spent on various recreational and leisure activities. Americans appear to be seeking more physically active recreation like bicycling, tennis, jogging and dancing.

There are various reasons, including increased leisure, population mobility and the huge population bulge of so many young people who were born during the post-WWII baby boom and who are now in their active adulthood. Commercial properties such as ski slopes, tennis centers and marinas are suburban-urban evidences of this trend. Probably more than in most other major industries, investing in land or buildings for commercial recreation means dealing with high-demand, high-profit, but sometimes "trendy," sometimes "faddish" manifestations. These changing recreation and leisure trends often take people out of movie houses and onto tennis courts, away from bowling alleys and onto ski slopes, out of skating rinks and into discos and racquetclubs. There's big money to be made quickly in recreational commercial properties, but these trendy risks have to be carefully evaluated and taken into account through careful analysis (see Chapter 7 for commercial location guidelines) and by *higher rent and profit returns to discount these risks.*

HOW TO PROFIT FROM SUNBELT GROWTH AND INDUSTRIAL PROPERTIES

If you want to make money from industrial real estate, you have to know what's happening in the region and in your local area. In the last 20 years, the number of manufacturing establishments rose in the South and Southwest and declined in the Northeast and Midwest. These older northern and midwestern sections suffer from high energy costs, cold climates, obsolete transportation systems and obsolete industrial plants. When you deal in land or building for industry, you have to know and check out the following:

- *Growth or decline area.* What are the regional trends?
- *Taxes, utilities.* Do tax assessment policies favor industrial or residential properties? Is tax abatement offered to industry? What is the local electrical kilowatt cost for industrial use?
- *Transportation.* Location and condition of road network? Railroad available? Rail costs?
- *Population trends.* Young people, labor force moving in or away?
- *Competitive businesses.* Have they have been moving into area or away to greener pastures which offer more advantages? Many vacant industrial plants in area? Are there counter trends, such as foreign industries coming into a declining Northeast region?

All these factors have to be considered before you can expect to profit. Once you are satisfied with the area and location, you have to then check out the proposed or existing industrial building to make certain it will have continued universal appeal when and if its tenant vacates. Except for industrial parks, most industrial buildings are generally built to meet a specific functional need of an industrial user. This contrasts with commercial buildings, primarily built to secure rental return on investment, and with residences, mainly built for resale and profit on investment. Resale of industrial buildings after original user abandonment usually involves modification of the building for the new user. Often the sales price must be lowered to reflect the cost of such changed use, particularly if major structural changes are needed.

So the idea is to design buildings with universal appeal; usually one story, fireproofed, sprinklered if possible; with flexible layout; adequate electric service; adequate ceiling heights; efficient receiving, loading, processing, storage, shipping space; commensurate office space; proper column spacing with wide enough bays; adequate parking space and room for expansion.

A Case Study of Industrial Site Profits

There's money to be made in industrial real estate. I once bought ten acres of industrially zoned land from a farmer for $2000 an acre and sold it to an industrial developer for $7000 an acre. He bought it because he needed four of the acres for a warehouse he was under contract to build for a beer distributor. The developer sold the four acres to the distributor for $60,000 or $15,000 an acre and also built him a 20,000 square foot masonry building for $400,000. All these transactions (and profits) took place in less than 18 months.

HOW TO USE CONSTRUCTION COSTS
TO CHECK OUT INDUSTRIAL BUILDINGS

This same industrial warehouse building can also be used as an actual illustration showing how you can use costs the way a builder does to check out proposed industrial buildings.

This building was planned with concrete block walls, brick and aluminum front facade, poured concrete reinforced foundation on special spread footings, structure 22 feet high, 990 square feet of finished office space, loading dock, two overhead doors, no sprinklers, individual well and septic system, 400 Amp electrical service, suspended heaters, paved fenced parking area, building 100′ × 200′, 200,000 square feet.

COST ESTIMATE BREAKDOWN

Architect	$15,000	Steel	$49,000
Fill	25,000	Office finish	15,000
Excavating, grading	15,000	Painting	6,000
Septic, well	13,000	Hardware	8,000
Paving	32,000	Legal, permits	6,000
Fence	8,000	Loan interest	20,000
Foundation	22,000	Insurance	4,000
Concrete floor	28,000	Sub-total	$391,000
Masonry	63,000	Contingency & Overhead	
Front facade	10,000	(Job Overhead—8%)	$ 31,000
Roofing	34,000	General O.H. & Profit	
Plumbing	10,000	(20%)	$ 78,000
Doors	8,000	Total:	$500,000
		Square Foot Cost	$25

THE BOOM IN PROFESSIONAL OFFICE BUILDINGS

A Tale of Two Buildings

A successful dentist I know recently built a professional office building. He got a great buy on the land, paying only $17,000 for a cleared, urban renewal plot in a small city adequate for his proposed building, including ample room for parking. The building rose quickly and beautifully, 13,000 square feet, ready for occupancy as scheduled. But there was big trouble. Tenants were found for only 7000 square feet. You see, the successful dentist hired his son, fresh out of architecture school, to design the building. It turned out to be a beautiful but expensive Taj Mahal. It cost $65 a square foot or $850,000 (in the suburbs), to build. Tenants remain hard to find at the square-foot rentals needed to amortize and profit from such a building cost in this suburban area.

Another investor, a doctor, bought a 1½-acre site in another similar suburban location which is a trading center for a large area. He built a one-story building, good looking, medically functional for a variety of doctors, but not loaded with any extra architectural cost. The building came to $52 a square foot. Rentals were appropriately lower than in the first example. His 11,000-square-foot building space was fully rented before the building was completed. An extension for additional square feet is now being planned.

It's really not necessary or advisable to cash in on this boom in professional office buildings by hiring one's son, the architect. It's better to understand this boom and to touch all the feasibility bases on a hard-nosed business basis. Doctors, attorneys, accountants and other professionals rarely practice nowadays from their own homes or in small, individual office buildings. Usually in the suburbs, but now even in cities, designed and managed professional office buildings cater to professionals. In these buildings, often medical arts buildings, doctors of various specialties usually rent about 1200 feet (up) of space. Groups of doctors, the modern trend in medicine, also find this type of building convenient for practice. This type of medical building requires more plumbing, partitions, sophisticated heating/cooling, stain-resistent carpeting, and is more expensive to build than the usual office building (although usually not yet $65). Parking must be ample, site pleasantly landscaped, and location must have good road access. Sometimes these medical professional buildings are located near or on hospital leased grounds so that doctors don't lose time commuting to the hospital and can refer their patients to the hospital when indicated.

Also not only doctors, but many other types of professionals and corporate tenants are moving into old, sometimes historic, buildings, usually in or near town centers. Those buildings which have good location and enough room for parking are beginning to command high prices and, after conversion, offer very good rentals at high professional office space rates. Disenchanted with the typical plastic and aluminum new buildings, professional and corporate tenants like the ambiance of exposed beams and fine old woodwork restored and left open in 100-year-old frame mansions converted to modern professional offices. This is a unique, excellent investment opportunity for investors who know their own locale. (More on this in Chapter 12 on conversions and renovations.)

An indication of the need for and the quality nature of this boom in professional medical office buildings is that banks generally rate such tenants "triple-A" in terms of financing mortgages on such buildings. (U.S. government agency tenants are also rated "triple-A.")

There's a boom on in professional office buildings, especially in local suburban-exurban areas. This is how you do the necessary feasibility analysis:

HOW TO ANALYZE OFFICE BUILDING SITES

- *Research the market.* Identify prospective tenants, tenant requirements as well as typical size of offices needed.

- *Analyze the area.* Identify population and economic trends; check out existing and proposed competition.
- *Forecast the rental period needed.* Estimate the time needed to absorb the square footage proposed.
- *Study the proposed site.* Analyze the site in terms of its location, accessibility, topography, dimensions, subsurface, zoning, utilities, and neighborhood influences.
- *Project land and construction costs.*
- *Project cash flow.*
- *Project operating costs.* Consider tax aspects also.
- *Check for appropriate design.* Are layout and appearance appropriate for prospective tenants, including special facilities and amenities for special type office buildings?

LOCAL KNOWLEDGE PAYS OFF

In sum, these are all the modern ways the pros are cashing in on commercial and industrial properties. If you use your local knowledge and contacts in your area and all these guidelines, you too can get in on this big boom in these little-known commercial and industrial investments.

10

Mini-Warehouses: How to Cash In on New Industrial Storage Facilities That Serve Modern Lifestyles

This entire chapter is on the mini-warehouse, that especially appropriate solution to the storage problems of our modern lifestyles. You'll find here how to make big profits from these little-known light industrial buildings that are just beginning to supply the tremendous modern-day suburban-urban housing and small business demand for additional, reasonable, secure storage space. Step-by-step procedures are detailed which give you all the keys to successful location, construction, conversion and operation of mini-warehouses. There is a feasibility-cost analysis-appraisal section that shows you how to ensure quick payout and continuing high profits by stressing low construction, improvement and operation cost features contrasted with the high square-foot rentals returned by these mini-warehouse cubicles. Finally, there is a mini-warehouse building sketch series that illustrates the infinite variety of interior cubicles that can be designed to satisfy profitably every local storage need.

HOW TO PROFIT FROM THIS MODERN-DAY
NEED FOR EXTRA STORAGE SPACE

What is the mini-warehouse? It is a light industrial building complex servicing modern lifestyles. It is a moneymaker. It could also become your maxi-profit operation if you build, buy or convert a mini-warehouse right—in the right place.

The mini-warehouse concept began in the Southwest and is needed in all regions. This new type of light industrial building is always a one-story structure, often of prefabricated metal, sometimes of site-built masonry. It has to be economical to erect and functional to operate in order to make money. It is distinguished from all other types of industrial buildings by its many interior partitioned cubicles and exterior doors. Best and most important of all, it is built "wholesale," of reasonable, modular, repetitive design and materials, but rented "retail" at *much higher than average* warehouse square-foot rentals. These higher rentals, averaging about $5 per square foot annually, come about because comparatively small cubicles of warehouse space are rented at these "retail" rates.

The renters are apartment owners who have inadequate space for storage in their apartments; small merchants with excess inventory; mail-order businessmen who need space for their stock; small contractors who must store tools, material and equipment; mobile home owners; people in the process of moving; even small-home owners who need additional storage space. Military personnel rent these spaces. Some small contractors who work out of their homes rent these cubicles to comply with state licensing requirements that they have a business address in a non-residential location. Some people use the spaces for shopwork, for car repairs and for tools and material storage. Actually, anyone who doesn't have a large, dry basement or easily accessible attic with beams sized for storage can use a mini-warehouse unit.

The mini-warehouse is basically a one-story building or complex of buildings divided into cubicles ranging from about 25 to 600 square feet each. (See photo and Figure 10-1, at end of chapter.) The site should be surrounded by a security fence and protected by watchmen and/or a resident manager. Some mini-warehouse complexes are open all the time; others from 6:00 A.M. to midnight. To cope with local needs and growth, they should be designed for expansion. The number of rental cubicles ranges up to 700 and the buildings should be built of fireproof or fire-resistant masonry or metal.

The buildings normally have no water or sewer service and are not heated. Some are not even lighted on the interior. All have security exterior lighting. Rental unit sizes usually range from 25 to 600 square feet. Small cubicles have their own exterior three-foot door. Larger spaces are equipped with overhead exterior garage doors. All doors are hasped for locking, usually by the tenant's own padlock.

The units rent for as little as $15 a month to as much as $225 per month. Turnover and vacancy rates are comparatively high because of the nature of the tenancy. But total annual rentals are comparatively very high because of this very same type of tenancy and nature of the rental space. Gross annual average rentals are about $5 per square foot. In well-located mini-warehouses, this high rental produces extraordinarily high net profits. Income tax write-off is also very high because of the type of building.

So the old profit adage, "Build or buy cheap, rent dear," is especially appropriate to this unique, little-known mini-warehouse idea. The feasibility-cost analysis-appraisal sections that follow detail how you too can profit from this new concept.

THE KEYS TO SUCCESSFUL LOCATION
AND OPERATION OF MINI-WAREHOUSES

As in practically all real estate income properties, location is the major key to successful operation. This is true whether it be a vacant site for building, an existing industrial structure for conversion, or an existing mini-warehouse for purchase. To make big profits you must first have the right location. Here are the key criteria for your market feasibility study, site selection and design layout:

Step 1. *Analyze the market.* Are there numerous apartment or condominium projects in the vicinity? Are there mobile home parks nearby? Are there shopping centers in the area with many small satellite stores without cellars and limited storage for inventory? Is there a military base nearby? Are there many low-to-moderate-income small home developments in the area with inadequate storage for interior and exterior items? Are there recreational lakes or waterways or oceanfront in areas where trailered or off-season boat storage is needed? Is there a minimum of 40,000 population within a 15-minute drive? Of all these factors, the most important is the number of apartment and condominium residents in the area. This is the key factor. They are the most important tenants.

Step 2. *Analyze the site.* If proposed, is site level, well drained? Accessible by a good road? Utilities like water or sewer are not needed and cheaper industrially zoned land without utilities is therefore feasible for mini-warehouses. However, the site should be serviced by electricity for exterior security lighting for the mini-warehouses. Interior lights are installed only if there is market demand.

Step 3. Analyze existing or conversion complexes. If an *existing* mini-warehouse is considered for purchase, is the site fenced? Is the building masonry or metal? All drainage positive away from buildings and off site? Is the site well lighted for security? Paved circulation around buildings? Room for expansion? No ponding water after rains? Watchmen and manager controls efficient? Adequate exterior paved area for vehicle and boat storage?

If a *conversion* complex, does the land meet all the preceding site criteria? Are the buildings one story, of fireproof construction? Are there enough exterior garage and other doors for conversion? If not, do the buildings have exterior post and beam construction to permit reasonable installation of exterior doors? Are the spans of the building roofs either 20, 30, 40 or 48 feet and the heights of the buildings no more than about 15 feet so that interior partitioning can be done economically? (Spaces will have to be divided up into cubicles as small as 5' × 5' and in various sizes up to double 10' × 48' to meet market space and security demands.)

Step 4. Analyze the improvements. Inspect condition of buildings, of roofs, of exteriors, of doors, of interiors. Are there bearing partitions that will interfere with optimum flexible partition design? Are there columns that will be in the way? If the buildings are of metal construction, are there unrepaired damaged panels or structural members? If of masonry, is there any structural cracking, water entry? Are there adequate bumper guards where needed, particularly in light metal buildings?

Step 5. Analyze the operation. If *existing,* check tenancy records, turnover rate. Is vacancy rate higher than 15%? Is there 24-hour access? Is 24-hour access needed in area? Analyze the expenses and income. If *proposed or recently built,* project the operating expenses, taxes, insurance, maintenance and management expenses reserve for replacement and vacancy deduction. Deduct these expenses from anticipated gross rentals to secure net profit. (See later sections for cost-valuation analysis and examples.)

LOW CONSTRUCTION COST PLUS HIGH SQUARE-FOOT RENTALS YIELDS QUICK PAYOUT AND HIGH PROFITS

The profit arithmetic is simple. If your location is right, the site feasible, the buildings reasonable to build or alter and the demand there, you'll make money. For example, the arithmetic on one small mini-warehouse project I recently analyzed is as follows:

1. *DESCRIPTION.* 200 units, sized from 5′ × 5′ to 10′ × 30′ in five steel prefabricated buildings for a total of 22,500 square feet of buildings on three acres of land zoned for light industry. No water, sewer, heat or interior lights in buildings. Site has 1½ acres paved and fenced. It is well drained. There are exterior security lights. Gates are locked from midnight to 6:oo A.M. A resident manager is the only employee, receiving salary, living quarters and utilities. Operation of mini-warehouse is strictly storage; no boat or car repairs permitted. Road access to the site is by a good county road.

2. *RAW LAND, IMPROVEMENT AND CONSTRUCTION COSTS*
2½ Acres land @ $8000 ....$20,000
Paving (1½ acres); fencing (950′).............................$40,000
Prefab metal buildings
22,500 SF @ $12.50 (installed)........................... .275,000
TOTAL COST..$335,000

3. *GROSS INCOME*

NO. UNITS	SIZE	MONTHLY RATE	MONTHLY TOTAL
10	5×5	$14	$140
40	5×10	22	880
10	5×15	30	300
50	10×10	36	1800
30	10×15	55	1650
40	10×20	60	2400
10	10×25	70	700
10	10×30	80	800
TOTALS 200	—	—	$8670

ANNUAL GROSS INCOME — ($8670 × 12) = $104,000

The numbers on this comparatively small mini-warehouse complex are revealing. Gross income is very high compared to the cost and investment. To estimate the current value of this property, we use the income approach to capitalize projected net income derived from the gross rentals. Net income is secured by deducting operating expenses including salaries, supplies, utility costs, taxes, insurance, maintenance, reserve for replacement, management expenses and vacancy rates from the (projected) gross rentals. This net income is then capitalized for this recently built complex by using straight-line depreciation plus a capitalization rate appropriate for this type of property. Since light construction and high rental turnover is usually involved in mini-warehouses, comparatively fast depreciation (ranging down to 20 years) and high capitalization rates (ranging up to 16%) are usually used. Valuation analysis of this property is as follows:

(PROJECTED) GROSS INCOME	$104,000
EXPENSES:	
Supplies (salt, brooms)	$300
Management	15,000
Advertising	2,000
Utilities (exterior lights, telephone)	2,200
Maintenance (snow removal, repairs)	2,000
Taxes	8,500
Reserve for replacement	6,000
Vacancy rate (9%)**	10,000
Total Expenses	$50,000
NET INCOME	$54,000

**(Actual vacancy rate for this mini-warehouse was a startling low 4% after only one year of operation. There are 50 more units being added now.)

Capitalization rate of 13.5% has been built up for this mini-warehouse complex from analysis of the first mortgage of 60% at 9½% interest which equals 5.7% when multiplied out; owner's equity of 40% at 8% interest equals 3.2%; 22-year life equals 4.6% depreciation for a total capitalization rate of 13.5%.

$(5.7\% + 3.2\% + 4.6\% = 13.5\%$ Cap. Rate)

Considering the age, location, condition and rising growth demand in this location, this capitalization rate of 13.5% appears justified by market analysis also.

Thus:
$54,000 (Net Income) ÷ 13.5% (Cap. Rate) = $400,000 (Value)

Therefore, by our income approach appraisal analysis, we have determined that the current value of the property after only about 18 months of operation is $400,000, an approximate 20% capital gain from its original cost of $335,000. The high net income of $54,000 annually before mortgage service is also an excellent return on the comparatively low original cost and investment. This example not only shows how to value mini-warehouses by the income approach but it also demonstrates the financial success such a well-located, well-designed (even if comparatively) small mini-warehouse can expect in an area of good demand.

THE "BOTTOM LINE" ON PROFITS IN
MINI-WAREHOUSES

The foregoing was one of the first mini-warehouses built in the Northeast. This particular investor utilized part of his own land which had been lying vacant. (Land value—$8,000 per acre per above project data.) He thus found this an excellent income-producing use for his land. He also found himself netting $60,000 a year profit (before mortgage service expenses of $20,000) on a cash investment of only $125,000. This was after only one year of operation with a startlingly low actual vacancy rate of 4%. It is a striking example of how one wide-awake investor is cashing in high net profits of almost *33% annually,* not even counting accelerated tax write-off, from this little-known, local, modern-day mini-warehouse profit opportunity.

In sum, the idea of mini-warehouses is good for profits because:

• *First:* It satisfies the growing storage demand caused by our modern lifestyle involving more compact shelter as well as business needs.

• *Second:* It needs comparatively cheap industrially zoned land because public sewer and water are not necessary.

• *Third:* It can be built with comparatively cheap structures, without mechanical utilities like water, sewer and heat. Often, even interior lighting is not needed.

• *Fourth:* It can be operated with a minimum of labor expense.

• *Fifth:* It suffers from no unusual bars to approval because of environmental restrictions or from additional building costs to eliminate pollution. Aside from some higher traffic count on an irregular basis, there is no industrial pollution caused by mini-warehouses.

• *Sixth:* It earns high net income because the spaces rented are small on a unit basis. So even though the total overall square foot rates are high, the comparatively small cubicles make for low enough monthly rent to attract tenants.

• *Seventh:* As shown in the example, the value of a mini-warehouse is based on its rents or the return on investment it generates, not on its low cost to build. In other words, in estimating mini-warehouse investment and profits, it's not what you put into it—it's where you put it and the excellent profits you get out of it that counts.

By all these criteria and for all these reasons, the mini-warehouse is an excellent, unique real estate profit opportunity. You too can cash in on this modern industrial usage if you follow the action plans detailed in the preceding sections on market, site, building feasibility investigation and analysis.

TRADE ASSOCIATION AND
OTHER INDUSTRY AID

A trade association called the Self-Service Storage Association assists its mini-warehouse owner and associate members in various ways. It focuses on areas such as marketing, advertising, construction, accounting, taxes, legal, financing, labor, security, operating procedure and insurance. It has regional organizations and its national address is:

> Self-Service Storage Association
> 1406 Third National Building
> Dayton, Ohio 45402   513/223-0419

Prefabricators like Trachte Metal Buildings Co. of 102 N. Dickenson St., Madison, Wis. 53703, phone (608) 257-3676, use special design building systems to produce and deliver efficient, attractive mini-warehouses.

A MINI-WAREHOUSE BUILDING SKETCH SERIES

The handy mini-warehouse sketch series presented here (photograph and Figure 10-1) graphically illustrates the many variable interior cubicle layouts that can be designed to meet varying local storage needs.

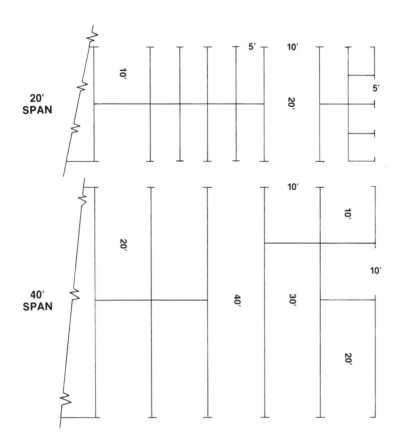

FIGURE 10-1: Mini-Warehouse Sketch Series
Showing Cubicles 5' × 5', 5' × 10',
10' × 10', 10' × 20', 10' × 30', 10'
× 40' in 20' × 40' span buildings.
(Scale - 1" = 10')

11

How to Make Money in Unusual Residential Real Estate Deals

This chapter deals specifically with residential real estate investments. There is a section on how to make big profits quickly whenever residential supply is tight. You are shown how the one-family house and its spin-off, the two-family, are still where you find great, sometimes tax-free, profit. The modern American phenomenon, our era of the "singles" with its impact on residential deals and profits, is detailed. Various little-known, local, unique ways to make money in houses are then shown: how to buy and fix up old homes in cities . . . how to make big profits from dealing in new houses in "slow suburbs" . . . how to recognize good construction in houses. Finally, there is a section on how to work with and profit from government regulations.

HOW TO MAKE BIG PROFITS QUICKLY
DURING TIGHT RESIDENTIAL TIMES

Some years ago, Doctor C. bought a 2850-square foot house in the pleasant Southern California peninsula town of _____ for $70,000 with $10,000 down. While he lived there, he added a pool and some other improvements for $12,000. A year later, he sold it for $120,000. He liked living on that hilly coastal peninsula, so he took the proceeds from the first house and bought a 4000-square-foot house nearby for $220,000. The pool and other improvements he installed on this house added $35,000. He sold the property for $420,000 in 1978. Still in the same vicinity but on a higher plot with better views of the ocean, he bought a one-acre plot for $120,000 and built a 5000-square-foot house on it, costing $330,000. He is living there now. He was recently offered and turned down *a million dollars* for the property.

A fantastic but very real story. It deals not just with the effects of inflation. This homeowner far outstripped inflation in pyramiding his original $10,000 down payment and $82,000 parcel in six years into a million-dollar property. It also shows how he "rode up" on the housing value boom in this tight Southern California market where demand for homes far outstripped supply. It also demonstrates these other successful ways to make money in residential housing:

The Doctor's "Pyramiding" Analyzed

• The one-family home is one investment where you get to eat your cake and still have it. Each time he sold his house for fantastic profits, he didn't even have to charge himself rent for all the time he had lived in the house.

• Location was the key factor in his very high profits. Southern California housing was in great demand compared to supply. His particular coastal peninsula became a "gold coast" while its inhabitants watched resale values rise spectacularly as supply of new construction lagged far behind. What this homeowner did was buy or build each time on a progressively higher hill plateau to make his value plateau even higher.

• The supply and demand factor was also critical here. Not too many buildable plots were left on this peninsula. There were too many buyers for what was available.

HOW TO PROFIT FROM MODERN SHELTER AND LIFESTYLES

Whether it be the above-cited $80,000 small house transformed by investment into a million dollar "gold coast" property, a condominium apartment, a suburban tract house skyrocketing in value or an urban row house converted into a townhouse, the name of the profit game for Americans today is home ownership. Inflation appears to be robbing money of its value. A home on land doesn't disappear as money does.

For whatever reason, profit or an even more elemental need, the middleclass family of today wants to own a home. The modern single man or woman also wants to own a home. More and more people are buying houses for investment purposes. They have observed that house values have gone up steadily in the last two decades while other investments like the stock market have fluctuated, often downwards. Tax advantages have always been there on the sale of homes. Recently, they've gotten spectacularly better.

$100,000 TAX-FREE
FOR RETIREES

You don't have to get a medical degree to profit from residences. If you're 55 (or planning for when you will be 55) or older, the Revenue Act of 1978 grants you freedom from income taxes up to $100,000 on capital gain profits from sale of homes. It sounds astounding but there are countless people who qualify or will qualify to make this $100,000 tax free. In ten years, housing prices have more than doubled!

For example, Mr. and Mrs. W. of San Francisco bought their first home 22 years ago. As their family and income increased they kept trading up to bigger and costlier homes. Each time, higher housing prices gave them big profits which they invested in their next house. Tax laws state that if you reinvest these profits in another house within 18 months, you can defer payment of the taxes. Now this last house they own is worth over $175,000 and they are selling it. Their family is grown and out of the house. Only $3000 of their $103,000 profit will be taxed! And they plan to buy and move into a smaller, less expensive house with lower real estate taxes and less maintenance cost. The $100,000 profit will be put into investments to help support their retirement later. Also, this latest, much smaller house will start the whole profit process over again, even if capital gain taxes have to be paid. (Small moderate-price homes appreciate in value much faster than more expensive houses.) It's true. A house is not just a home. It has become the best investment you can make.

HOW SINGLES PROFIT FROM
ONE-FAMILY HOMES

It's also not just doctors and retirees and their families who can make it big in residential profits. There are 55,000,000 single adults in

America, many of whom are doing it too. For example, one of them, a young, tennis-playing woman attorney only two years out of law school, recently bought a 1400-square-foot one-story, six-room house in the San Fernando valley for $72,000. This was at the lower end of the value spectrum in California where average home prices exceed $100,000. What does a single person need with six rooms and a two-car garage? This single woman, like millions of others, reasoned from her work as an associate in a law firm specializing in real estate that a one-family house was her best bet for inflation tax hedge and future profit. She was not wrong. Three months after she moved in, the next-door neighbor who had taught her how to change faucet washers decided to sell his similar home. She helped him negotiate a sale equivalent to $89,000. (Buyer paid the real estate commission.) So this single woman now knows how to change washers—and maintain her home. Her neighbor has moved out with his $60,000 profit, (original cost $29,000 six years earlier.) And after only one year of ownership, she sold her own home for $102,000, for a $30,000 profit!

This true profit story is becoming typical of the life style of young middle-class America. The mere fact that you're single doesn't mean you can't get in on the boom in one-family resale profits. If you're a builder, it means you have to learn to work with and sell to single people. Banks have recognized this trend (with 25% of all homes being bought by singles), and are now financing this housing phenomenon with mortgages that in the past were usually denied to single people.

Bachelor Buys Two-Family Home

Sometimes it's not just one-family homes being snapped up by single people. In one suburban area, a bachelor in his late twenties bought a two-family house because he had figured out that the rental income would enable him to live cheaper than in the small apartment he had been renting—and still wind up with a valuable property to later resell. This two-family type of residential property is an especially little-known local real estate investment because most communities have at least one central area where zoning permits two-family homes, usually in older sections. Occasionally, a variance is permitted in other sections for a mother or married children. Most conversions of one-family into two-family dwellings take place through this zoning loophole. Sometimes, since they are in muliple zones, it even makes sense to convert existing two-family houses to condominiums and sell each of them for more than you can realize by selling the whole two-family house.

These modern techniques can be used by single (and married) people to profit from one-family and two-family homes. The residence boom is here and is continuing despite and because of the fact that the modern American family has become smaller and in many cases is not even a family.

Real estate is one of the few remaining chances for big profits. This is also still another investment area where local knowledge and contacts pay off. That doctor homeowner hung in there; the retiree made his retirement possible; that single person stayed way ahead of inflation. They all bought and built based on location, demand and local knowledge.

THE ONE-FAMILY HOME IS STILL WHERE THE MAIN ACTION IS

The one-family dwelling on its own lawn basically remains the "American dream house" despite counteracting land and construction cost inflation. The single family home still leads the suburban sales market. There's no longer any doubt that big profits in real money compared to inflation can be made and kept in one-family home deals.

However, you have to touch all the bases to make these big profits. You must be able to recognize and appraise current and potential value when you see it locally. You also have to be able to check out and recognize quality or unacceptable construction before you invest. If you buy a house with a basement or plot that floods or one riddled with termites, you may wind up losing your investment rather than making profits. Up to 25% of all new homes have serious problems like poor foundations, crumbling chimneys and leaky roofs. There are various warranty programs like "HOW" (Homeowner's Warranty Program) which a number of builders offer, insuring against serious defects for up to ten years. This should be investigated. To be forewarned is to be forearmed. The profits are there if you are careful. The checklist shown in Figure 11-1 can be taken along when you inspect a prospective property. Or you can hire an expert inspector to give you a report. His inspection should cover these same basic items.

CHARACTERISTICS OF PROPERTY (Proposed or existing construction)

Neighborhood

Consider each of the following to determine whether the location of the property will satisfy your personal needs and preferences:

Remarks

Convenience of public transportation
Stores conveniently located
Elementary school conveniently located
Absence of excessive traffic noise
Absence of smoke and unpleasant odors
Play area available for children
Fire and police protection provided
Residential usage safeguarded by adequate zoning

Lot

Consider each of the following to determine whether the lot is sufficiently large and properly improved:

Size of front yard satisfactory
Size of rear and side yards satisfactory
Walks provide access to front and service entrances
Drive provides easy access to garage
Lot appears to drain satisfactorily
Lawn and planting satisfactory
Septic tank (if any) in good operating condition
Well (if any) affording an adequate supply of safe and
    palatable water

Exterior Detail

Observe the exterior detail of neighboring houses and determine whether the house being considered is as good or better in respect to each of the following features:

Porches
Terraces
Garage
Gutters
Storm sash
Weather stripping
Screens

FIGURE 11-1: Characteristics of Property
                     (Proposed or Existing Construction)

Interior Detail

Consider each of the following to determine whether the house will afford living accommodations which are sufficient to the needs and comfort of your household:

Remarks

Rooms will accommodate desired furniture
Dining space sufficiently large
At least one closet in each bedroom
At least one coat closet and one linen closet
Convenient access to bathroom
Sufficient and convenient storage space (screens,
 trunks, boxes, off-season clothes, luggage, baby
 carriage, bicycle, wheel toys, etc.)
Kitchen well arranged and equipped
Laundry space ample and well located
Windows provide sufficient light and air
Sufficient number of electrial outlets

CONDITION OF EXISTING CONSTRUCTION

Exterior Construction

The following appear to be in acceptable condition:

Wood porch floor and steps
Windows, doors, and screens
Gutters and wood cornice
Wood siding
Mortar joints
Roofing
Chimneys
Paint on exterior woodwork

CAUTION: Cracking, peeling, scaling and loose paint on stairs, decks, porches, railings, windows and doors may contain amounts of lead which are harmful if eaten by children under seven years of age. Examine areas carefully.

Interior Construction

Plaster is free of excessive cracks
Plaster is free of stains caused by leaking roof or
 sidewalls
Door locks in operating condition

FIGURE 11-1 (continued)

Windows move freely
Fireplace works properly
Basement is dry and will resist moisture penetration
Mechanical equipment and electrical wiring and
    switches adequate and in operating condition
Type of heating equipment suitable
Adequate insulation in walls, floor, ceiling or roof

The following appear to be in acceptable condition:

Wood floor finish
Linoleum floors
Tile floors—vinyl asbestos, asphalt
Sink top
Kitchen range
Bathroom fixtures
Painting and papering
Exposed joists and beams

FIGURE 11-1 (continued)

HOW TO BUY, THEN RENT, NEW HOUSES IN "SLOW" SUBURBS

While it is true that *average* dwelling prices have surged ahead in our nation, millions of different sales at differing higher and lower prices in different localities go to make up this soaring average. All have generally been going up—in some areas at fantastic rates, in others at slow to very slow rates. There are areas where new home sales are very slow, as in many localities in the still economically depressed Northeast and Midwest.

Often, a development builder cannot just sit and watch his hoped-for profits and investment disappear while he waits to sell his new tract houses. He has financed their construction usually with high-interest interim construction loans which soon eat up anticipated profits if the units don't sell readily.

This is where profit opportunities also lie. Even in practically all economically depressed areas, there is a shortage of homes and apartments. If you locate such a new home or homes in your local area, this is how you proceed:

• *Location.* Look for good location with no local influences adverse to residential usage.

- *Valuation.* Appraise or have it appraised for current market value. (See Chapter 5.)
- *Inspection.* Inspect or have it inspected for construction. Try to get a warranty on the home if possible. (See previous chapter sections.)
- *Financing.* If it checks out, arrange for a mortgage, either through the builder or your own bank.
- *Make an offer.* Sometimes, depending on how slow the market is, a lower offer may be accepted.
- *Rent the house.* Even in slow areas, rents are usually high enough to carry most of the home costs.
- *Sell the house.* When the market, even in slow areas, has moved up enough to give you a good profit, sell.
- *Tax aspects.* If you hold it long enough, at least a year and a half to be certain, your profit should be taxed at capital gain rates. Also, while you hold it, the building can be depreciated because it is being rented and you can deduct interest and taxes.

As ever, this buy-rent-sell technique should be based on local knowledge of market conditions, carefully applied. In such investments, you are capitalizing and profiting from what normally would be a slow real estate situation.

This same buy-rent-sell technique can also be used in fast as well as slow selling areas. Investors have made fortunes in California and other areas, buying up new (and resale) one-family houses and then renting and holding them for profit resale. The same careful location, appraisal, inspection, financing, rental, resale procedure is followed with the possible exception of negotiating significantly lower purchase prices because an active sales market usually precludes "sacrifice" buys.

HOW TO WORK WITH AND PROFIT
FROM GOVERNMENT REGULATIONS

Federal government policies and agencies have a critical impact on real estate. Government housing and monetary policies have in recent years helped to make or break the housing industry and sometimes the whole economy. If you want to profit from real estate investment, you have to keep up with what's happening because of government financing and other agency actions and policies. You can also get invaluable help from many agencies, often at little or no cost. Here is a list of different agencies and how they can help you:

U.S. Superintendent of Documents, Washington, D.C. Once you write to the Superintendent to get on this list of government publications, he will send you regular mailings that list all recent publications by all agencies. You can then order those you need at very nominal cost. This mailing list will help keep you alert of all types of data on housing and real estate.

Department of Census. This is the single most important source of vital population statistics and for various useful studies on household formation and other important statistics.

Housing and Urban Development (HUD). This big housing agency, which incorporates the Federal Housing Administration (FHA), has available building codes, topical publications like Standards for Solar Heating, and flood maps, and offers various housing financing programs including modern innovative ones like Variable Rate Mortgages. The FHA also has lists available regularly of its foreclosed houses in all areas, which it offers for sale in "as-is" and repaired condition. A list of HUD regional offices is shown at the end of this chapter.

Veterans Administration. Like HUD, the VA is also still an important agency for veteran home financing. It also sells foreclosed houses. (See also Chapter 13 on foreclosures.)

Department of Commerce. This agency publishes a monthly review which summarizes economic trends and housing reports.

Environmental Protection Agency (EPA). This newest agency is a major source for data on pollution involving solid waste, air, water, pesticides, radiation and noise. Such up-to-date data is vital today for real estate investment in land for development.

Farmers Home Administration (FmHA), Department of Agriculture. The FmHA makes home and farm loans. The parent agency, the Department of Agriculture, can give valuable help, information and data. For example, there is an extreme shortage of one-family *small* homes in practically all exurban areas. The Forest Service of the Department of Agriculture has 11 different small home plans which can be built at comparatively low cost in exurban areas. See plan in Figure 11-2. Investors, builders and prosective homeowners can get working plans on 11 such designed homes for very nominal fees by writing to the Superintendent of Documents, Washington, D.C., using a copy of the order blank shown in Figure 11-3.

House Plan no. FS-FPL-5

AREA = 672 sq. ft. expandable to 1042 sq. ft.

Plan FS-FPL-5 provides for the construction of either a single-story two-bedroom home or an expandable type with two additional bedrooms on the second floor. The basic house is 24 by 28 feet in size with an area of 672 square feet. The expandable plan provides an additional area of about 370 square feet on the second floor. The second-floor bedrooms can be completed with the rest of the house or left unfinished until later. Both plans include a kitchen, bath, living room, and two bedrooms on the first floor.

To accommodate the stairway to the second-floor bedrooms in the expandable plan, the first-floor bed-

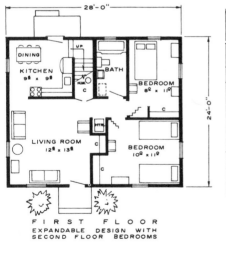

FIGURE 11-2

rooms and the kitchen are slightly smaller than those in the one-story plan. One second-floor bedroom is 9-1/2 by 14 feet and the other is 13 by 14 feet. The larger bedroom may be divided by the addition of a wardrobe wall, which provides two closets and also serves as a room divider.

Both plans have a front entrance closet and a closet for each bedroom. The expandable house also has a storage area under the stairway in which the hot water heater is located. The heating unit is located in a small closet adjacent to the bath-bedroom hallway. Walls, floors, and ceiling areas are insulated. Dining space is provided for in each kitchen.

This plan was developed by the Forest Products Laboratory of Madison, Wis., and is one of a series of plans for low-cost houses of wood being designed by the Forest Service, U.S. Department of Agriculture.

There are a number of factors which aid in reducing the cost of these homes. They are designed as crawl-space houses with post or pier foundations, which eliminate the need for extensive grading on sloping building sites. The single floor covering serves as a base for resilient tile or a low-cost linoleum rug. It can be painted if further cost reductions are required. Panel siding is used for exterior wall finish which eliminates sheathing and the need for a braced wall. Exteriors are finished with long-lasting pigmented stains. Many contrasting colors are available in this type of finish. Exterior and interior trim and millwork have been reduced to a minimum. However, many of these refinements can be made at anytime after the house has been completed.

Details of a second-floor bathroom, a porch addition, a full foundation wall, and an enclosing skirtboard are also included in the working drawings.

Designed By L. O. Anderson
Forest Products Laboratory

FIGURE 11-2 (continued)

Order Blank

Superintendent of Documents
U.S. Government Printing Office
Washington, D.C. 20402

Date .... , 19.......

Name ....

Street Address ....

City and State .... ZIP Code ....

FOR OFFICE USE ONLY	
Quantity	Charges
.... Enclosed	....
.... To be mailed	....
.... Subscriptions	
Postage	
Foreign handling	....
MMOB	
OPNR	....
.... UPNS	
.... Discount	
.... Refund	

MAIL ORDER FORM WITH REMITTANCE TO:

Superintendent of Documents, U.S. Government Printing Office, Washington, D.C. 20402

Enclosed find $............................ *(check or money order), or charge to my Deposit Account Number.*

Deposit Account Number

| | | | | | | | – | |

Your Order Number............................

Please send me the publications I have indicated below:

Stock No.	Qty.	Unit of Issue		Title	Unit Price	Total
001–001–00009–4	_____	set	FPL–1	(9 sheets)	$2.95	_____
001–001–00010–8	_____	set	FPL–2	(9 sheets)	2.95	_____
001–001–00011–6	_____	set	FPL–3	(8 sheets)	2.80	_____
001–001–00012–4	_____	set	FPL–4	(9 sheets)	2.95	_____
001–001–00008–6	_____	set	FPL–5	(10 sheets)	3.10	_____
001–001–00013–2	_____	set	SE–1	(6 sheets)	2.40	_____
001–001–00014–1	_____	set	SE–2	(4 sheets)	2.30	_____
001–001–00015–9	_____	set	SE–3	(5 sheets)	2.40	_____
001–001–00016–7	_____	set	SE–4	(7 sheets)	2.70	_____
001–001–00017–5	_____	set	SE–5	(6 sheets)	2.55	_____
001–001–00018–3	_____	set	SE–6	(6 sheets)	3.00	_____
001–001–00019–1	_____	ea.	Designs for Low-Cost Wood Homes		.50	_____
001–001–00747–5	_____	ea.	Low-Cost Wood Homes for Rural America—Construction Manual		1.45	_____

NOTE: Overall dimensions of all plans (FPL 1–5 & SE 1–6) are 24″ x 18″—drawn to scale.

PLEASE DO NOT DETACH

FOR PROMPT SHIPMENT, PLEASE **PRINT OR TYPE** ADDRESS ON LABEL BELOW, INCLUDING **YOUR ZIP CODE**

U.S. GOVERNMENT PRINTING OFFICE
SUPERINTENDENT OF DOCUMENTS
WASHINGTON, D.C. 20402

OFFICIAL BUSINESS

PENALTY FOR PRIVATE USE, $300

POSTAGE AND FEES PAID
U.S. GOVERNMENT PRINTING OFFICE
375
SPECIAL FOURTH-CLASS RATE
BOOK

Name _____

Street address _____

City and State _____ ZIP Code _____

CUT ALONG THIS LINE

FIGURE 11-3

HOUSING AND URBAN DEVELOPMENT
REGIONAL OFFICES

HUD Administration—Region I
Rm 800, John F. Kennedy Fed'l
Bldg.
Boston, Mass. 02203
Tel (203) 244-3638

HUD Administrator—Region II
26 Federal Plaza, Rm 3541
New York, N.Y. 10007
Tel (212) 264-8068

HUD Administrator—Region III
Curtis Building
6th & Walnut St.
Philadelphia, Pa. 19106
Tel (404) 526-5585

HUD Administrator—Region V
300 South Wacker Drive
Chicago, Illinois 60606
Tel (312) 353-5680

HUD Administrator—Region IV
Rm 211, Pershing Point Plaza
1371 Peachtree St., N.E.
Atlanta, Georgia 30309
Tel (404) 526-5585

HUD Administrator—Region VI
Earl Cabell Federal Building
U.S. Courthouse
1100 Commerce St.
Dallas, Texas 75242
Tel (214) 749-7401

HUD Administrator—Region VII
Federal Office Bldg—Rm 300
911 Walnut St.
Kansas City, Missouri 64016
Tel (816) 374-2661

HUD Administrator—Region VIII
Executive Tower
1405 Curtis St.
Denver, Colo 80202
Tel (303) 837-4513

HUD Administrator—Region IX
450 Golden Gate Ave
P.O. Box 36003
San Francisco, Calif. 94102
Tel (415) 556-4752

Regional Administrator
Arcade Plaza Bldg.
1321 Second Ave
Seattle, Washington 98101
Tel (206) 442-5414

12

Conversions and Renovations: How the Pros Are Making Big Money

This chapter is devoted entirely to property conversions and renovations. It shows you how the pros are making big money by converting and renovating rather than building new construction. It also shows how you too can get in on this high-profit recycling of older properties being done by "pioneers" in the cities and rehabbers in turnaround suburban neighborhoods. There is a section on "sweat equity" in brownstones. You are also given details on how to locate and profit from real "mechanic's specials" and from solar rehabilitation. Finally, there is a handy, illustrated, inspection guide for buying, fix-up and renovation profits.

HOW TO BUY AND FIX UP OLD HOMES IN CITIES

Many of the children of the white middle class which left the cities for the suburbs a generation ago are returning to the cities today. Many factors apply. This resurgence of deteriorated inner-city neighborhoods was led by urban pioneers. These pioneers were mainly young, affluent people seeking the diversity of urban life, but they also included "empty-nesters," older people, ethnics and middle-class black people. The skyrocketing cost of suburban housing made rehabilitation of sound urban buildings especially attractive and feasible. Cost of commuting from the suburbs to city jobs soared. This trend back to the cities has appeared everywhere and appears to be overcoming alleged mortgage "redlining." Bank financing has again become available for urban real estate properties in many areas. Revitalization of old rundown neighborhoods is taking place in New York City, Pittsburgh, Savannah, Ann Arbor, St. Louis, Washington, D.C., San Francisco and in many other cities.

As on one- and two-family houses in the suburbs, you can make money, plenty of money, in the cities on these urban one- to four-family buildings and even larger multiple dwellings if you recognize and evaluate these profit opportunities. This is how to do it. Know what's happening on a block-by-block neighborhood basis. There is a growing market, particularly among young people ages 25 to 35, for rehabilitated urban shelter. Rehabilitation of neighborhoods feeds upon prior rehabilitation. The word spreads among these young people as to which are the "in" neighborhoods. It is a social and housing phenomenon which, like the overall boom in housing, cannot be dismissed as transient. Attached row houses in rundown areas of Brooklyn, N.Y., which I appraised 15 years ago for $10,000, sell nowadays at $90,000 for the rundown shell or $200,000 up if rehabilitated.

Big money can be made from buying and fixing up buildings in cities. As always, local knowledge, contacts and investigation on a block-by-block basis are what pay off.

$50,000 Profit for Part-Time Remodeling

A part-time remodeler bought a one-story frame house on a narrow lot in an improving city neighborhood for $40,000 recently. He spent $30,000 sprucing up the interior and opening up the dwelling to its rebuilt, landscaped rear garden-patio area. He sold it for $120,000. Profit: $50,000 in less than a year.

Other urban pioneers are converting former manufacturing loft buildings into beautiful, high-ceiling apartments and duplex dwelling units. Three- to five-story, old attached one- and two-family buildings are being converted into three and four cooperative or condominium units for fantastic profit.

As real estate prices skyrocket in the suburbs, such cheaper, older city properties which can be remodeled for less are looking better and better. Sometimes, Federal Urban Rehabilitation loans at low interest are available for home remodeling. (See HUD list of regional offices in Chapter 11.)

Like these urban pioneers, you can use the following three-pronged approach to get in on these great profits from such urban rehabilitation.

A TRIPLE YARDSTICK FOR URBAN PROFITS

- *Location.* Location comes first. Always buy in neighborhoods that are on the way up and show that they are beginning to appeal to affluent young singles and couples.
- *Structural soundness.* Building must be structurally sound and able to accommodate interior and exterior overhaul. (See inspection guide in last section of this chapter.)
- *Price.* The price must be right and the financing available. Alleged "redlining" is apparently lessening and bank mortgages are becoming available again in many city neighborhoods.

WHERE TO GET FINANCING
FOR CONVERSIONS AND RENOVATIONS

- **Conventional Mortgages from Institutions**
  1. Savings banks.
  2. Commercial banks.
  3. Savings and Loan Associations.
  4. Building and Loan Associations.
  5. Title and Trust Companies.
  6. Mortgage companies who represent individuals, banks, insurance companies and other institutional lenders.

- **Government-Backed Mortgages from Institutions**
  1. V.A. guaranteed loans for veterans housing.
  2. F.H.A.-H.U.D. insured housing loans.

- **Direct Government Loans to Purchasers**
  1. V.A. loans to all who buy V.A.-foreclosed properties.
  2. F.H.A. loans to all people who buy FHA-foreclosed properties.
  3. S.B.A. business loans.

- **Other and Little-Known Ways to Raise Money**
  1. *Assume* an existing mortgage.
  2. *Second mortgages* from banks.
  3. *First and second mortgages* from individuals.
  4. *Purchase money* mortgages from sellers.
  5. *Graduated payment mortgages* from banks to young people.
  6. *Variable rate mortgages* from banks tailored to meet inflation by permitting the interest rate on mortgages to move up and down during the life of the mortgages.

7. *Construction mortgages* from banks and other lenders.
8. *Installment or contract sales* of property. Seller does not give a deed to the buyer until buyer has paid in a certain percentage of the purchase price. Meanwhile buyer has control and use of the property, other than ownership.
9. *Options to purchase.*
10. *Lease with options to purchase.*
11. *Mortgages with special terms* like "interest only."
12. *Local syndication.*

How Rehabbers Spot the Turnaround Areas

A group of rehabbers in a small northwestern city recently remodeled three vacant buildings, two of them historic. They turned them into a very lively collection of downtown shops, restaurants and offices. Their judgment that this small downtown deteriorated city area had bottomed out and was ripe for turnaround rejuvenation proved profoundly correct. Many residents are apparently fed up with outlying shopping center sprawl and are flocking to this revitalized downtown center. The "bottom" profit line was also helped by 15-year tax abatement for the historic buildings.

How One Conversion Paid Off 21% Yearly

Another remodeler spotted a heavily vandalized, abandoned supermarket in a small suburban town. He bet that it was also a turnaround area and bought the 16,000-square-foot building for $150,000. He spent another $200,000 to convert it into a much needed small neighborhood multi-purpose shopping center. His bet paid off. A bank took 3000 square feet and a laundromat, post office and other speciality shops rented basic 14-foot wide storefronts for $6.50 a square foot. The payoff:

Acquisition and renovation costs..$350,000
Gross income (less 5% Vacancy) 90,000
Cash flow (net after expenses incl. mortgage payout)........... 15,000
Return on investment (net ÷ $70,000 equity) 21%
Tax aspects (see Chapter 4)...Tax write-off
and depreciation

KEY FACTORS FOR OFFICE BUILDING CONVERSIONS

Another imaginative suburban and urban profit bonanza is the rehabilitation of old mansions and their conversion into office buildings. (See also Chapter 9 on the boom in suburban professional office buildings.) These older properties usually have excellent downtown locations and are frequently situated on large lots which provide good parking. The idea here also is to study the location carefully, weighing its patterns of rehabilitation against the existing deterioration. Note whether the key indicators for turnaround sections are operating. Are the young affluent people coming back into the neighborhood? Have deterioration and economy of the area and location bottomed out? Are there other properties being rehabilitated in the vicinity? Again, local knowledge is most important in turnaround area. Big profits await the perceptive investor.

Examples of How to Recycle Office Buildings

An architect in Connecticut took a very large old but sturdy house and converted it into dramatic and beautiful offices for himself and for three other professional and corporate clients. The square-foot rentals are 50% more than nearby "modern" space.

A title company executive bought a rambling old Victorian building on three acres in a New York county seat town across the street from a county courthouse which had been recently built in a deteriorated urban renewal area. Office space in the old building, converted into offices for the title company and for various law firms, is now at a premium. The many lawyer-tenants like the idea of being able to walk across the street to the courthouse from their offices. The high square-foot rentals reflect this attractive location. Also, the success of this conversion has sparked other rehabilitation in nearby properties in this turnaround area.

HOW TO GET IN ON CONVERSION
AND RENOVATION PROFITS

There are big conversion and renovation profits, not just in the cities but also in the suburbs and rural exurbs . . . not just in residences but also in commercial and industrial properties . . . not just in conventional type of properties, but also in many types of unique little-known real estate parcels. These conversions and renovations are taking place now wherever it pays to buy and fix up or rebuild compared to the cost of new construction. They are also taking place in areas our young people seek in order to be where the urban action is. All these key indicators and factors are what you have to look for if you want to be successful and cash in on this explosive modern trend to conversion and renovation.

A unique example of such modern conversion is what you can make happen to abandoned schools in your area. As fewer children are born in our smaller families today, more and more schools are being made obsolete and are closing. What does one do with one- to three-story school buildings in city and suburban neighborhoods? A few have been turned into remodeled housing very successfully and profitably. There are many such reasonable white elephants that can be recycled into highly profitable housing, using the following step-by-step procedures:

CHECKLIST OF PROCEDURES
FOR CONVERTING SCHOOLS

• *Zoning.* Make sure the zoning permits the proposed use.
• *Location.* Check out all the basic location factors for housing usages.
• *Purchase or leasing.* Sometimes the local community will be interested in giving long leases on the property, particularly if it can help control tenancy or unit sale, such as to senior citizens.
• *Tax abatement.* Since these are public properties, tax abatements can often be negotiated, again if some or all of the units can be offered to special need tenants in the community. Often even without abatement, lower acquisition and conversion costs make such remodeled housing conventionally feasible.
• *Subsidy programs.* The Housing and Urban Development agency has various subsidy programs. Some states and communities have local programs which should be investigated. Again, even without subsidy, conventional conversion is often possible in many locations.
• *Syndication.* Financing of equity investment funds can sometimes be facilitated by syndicating such conversions to a number of local investors.
• *Building codes.* These have to be carefully analyzed for compliance.
• *Special features.* The high ceilings, wide hallways and old architectural details can often be utilized for additional apartments, duplex apartments and interesting, unusual, retained details.

Similar conversion to subsidized and conventional housing has also been done with older, abandoned hospitals. More and more hospitals are becoming surplus now as hospital costs soar and duplication of area hospital services becomes increasingly inefficient.

Whether it be such comparatively large school/hospital conversions to multiple housing in the city and suburbs or a converted small one-family townhouse (as detailed in the next chapter section), remodeling and conversion appear to be the real estate wave of the future. The earlier American building development approach of "demolish and build new" has evolved to "remodel and convert." As land costs skyrocket in the suburbs, many young Americans are turning back to existing buildings and neighborhoods. Local real estate knowledge is what pays off here too.

"SWEAT EQUITY" IN BROWNSTONES AND "MECHANIC'S SPECIALS"

There are many thousands of New York City attached one- to four-family row houses called "brownstones" (photo, page 150) because of the color of the exterior front masonry. There are similar attached frame and masonry houses in many other cities. Some of these buildings are historic; most were built around the turn of this century. Generally, there are fireplaces, hall pier mirrors, sliding doors, built-in china closets, wood wainscoting, parquet floors, stained woodwork. The buildings have mass, are suited for today's high energy costs, and are usually of very sturdy, superior construction. Many of these dwellings today would cost up to an estimated $750,000 to reproduce with the same fine handmade detailing! Yet many can still be bought for comparatively very little, particularly if they are in deteriorated condition in potentially turnaround neighborhoods.

In many cities, such brownstone-type areas have already been mainly rehabilitated by urban pioneers, often working without mortgages or with inadequate financing and using their own funds and "sweat" labor to create equity in their rehabilitated buildings. This "sweat equity" has revitalized whole neighborhoods, even in the midst of still abandoned buildings and buildings being rehabilitated. For example, of the 40-plus brownstone areas in New York City and nearby New Jersey, about 15 areas have already become so popular that it has become hard to find a building to rehabilitate. Renovated buildings in some of these areas sell for as much as $350,000. However, there are many hundreds of such inner-city and downtown-suburb deteriorated areas ripe for turnaround rehabilitation. Success in one block and one neighborhood spawns revitalization of adjoining blocks and neighborhoods. Watch for such trends in your local area. It's not just more examples of the dynamism inherent in real estate. It's cold business dollars-and-cents logic to capitalize on this modern, unique real estate trend and make big profits on this accelerating, changing urban way of life.

New is out; old is in. This modern phenomenon which appears

to describe what's been happening recently in so many city areas also applies to suburban-exurban regions. The "mechanic's special" so often seen in real estate ads is also becoming increasingly popular in suburban areas. The same push-pull factors of high land and construction cost are creating vast markets for recycled, modernized, older, rundown properties in the suburbs.

Not every building is worth remodeling. How do you evaluate

whether the existing property is past the point where it can be recycled for profit? How do you make sure, once you've judged that the location is good, or will be good, that the building on the site is not already past redemption? The "mechanic's special," often advertised so glibly, may not be worth the time of the mechanic investor. Yet big profits are there if the location is good and the bone structure of the building is sound. This is how you can hedge your investment bets and make sure you cash in on the "sweat equity" you create in remodeled properties. The *real* "mechanic's special" is the one that can pass the following location and inspection feasibility step-by-step procedure:

PRACTICAL TIPS ON "MECHANIC'S SPECIALS"

Step 1. Do a thorough inspection and analysis. If you believe that expert inspection help besides your own is necessary on a particular property, you should expect that the inspector's report will cover these same important points.

Step 2. Check location. This is paramount.

Step 3. Check for financing. Available?

Step 4. Review zoning and building codes. Is usage a conforming use? Is the projected remodeled use permissible by zoning and building codes?

Step 5. Inspect construction. Inspect for lot and block drainage, foundation, framing, windows, roof, interior, decay and insect damage, insulation, moisture control, utilities, heating, plumbing and electricity. (See following detailed section on inspection.)

Step 6. Value the property. Make sure the "mechanic's special" is the bargain it's advertised to be. Remember, after you determine its current value, depreciated for its deteriorated condition, you still have to renovate it. Remodeling costs are generally about twice as much as new construction.

HOW TO PROFIT FROM SOLAR
REHABILITATION

Solar energy is as old as the sun and as new as the energy crisis. Although solar energy technologies are still young and comparatively expensive, the rapidly inflating cost of oil and gas is making crash programs inevitable and profitable in solar energy utilization for conversions and renovations.

Another sign of these solar times is that San Diego recently became the first community to require domestic solar hot water installations on *all new* constructions. New law is even being made today in this very new real estate field. Zoning ordinances on preventing shade of solar installations are being written now and will have to be checked whenever you do solar rehabbing or new construction.

The government is spending billions to stimulate the development of solar heat as well as solar domestic hot water. The sun's energy is practically inexhaustible; oil is not. This is another vital illustration of the principle that for real estate profits you have to go where the action will be—and get there early.

A Case History of Solar Profits

Here's a working example of how one investor profited from such a conversion even at this very early stage. Alexander J. of New York City is in the business of renovating brownstone buildings into cooperatives. This is how local and federal tax incentives and energy savings are making profits for him now. His five-story townhouse building on the west side of Manhattan has had 12 solar collectors on its roof now for the past few years. These collectors have been supplying 65% of the annual energy needed to heat the building's hot water. This amounts to $500 annual savings. New York City's J51 law not only exempts the value-added improvements from real estate tax for 12 years, but also permits the property owner to deduct from his real estate tax 90% of the cost of improvements (8.3% per year over 12 years). In this case, his $6,000 solar system investment resulted in a deduction of still another $500 saved *each* year.

Add all this to a 10% investment tax credit, a depreciation allowance and a low-cost (9½%) energy loan from a local bank. Since this investor lives in one of the nine apartments, he was also able to take 30% residential energy credit on one-ninth of the total cost of the system, thanks to the National Energy Act. Based on his very successful two years of experience, this investor started two similar installations on other buildings.

A HANDY INSPECTION GUIDE FOR
RENOVATION PROFITS

The following inspection guide details the specific items to look for when you are considering buying and rehabilitating or remodeling an existing building. Many of the items pertain to frame buildings. However, the guide can also be generally applied to other types of construction as well. Illustrations in Figures 12-1 through 12-5 are taken from the U.S.D.A. Forest Service Bulletin No. 212, a good inspection booklet for checking out basic structures and nonstructural essentials. (See pages 154–157.)

RENOVATION INSPECTION GUIDE

KEY INSPECTION FACTORS

* Is foundation good?
* Is building square?
* Is building free from decay and insect damage?
* Is building layout acceptable or is it feasible to modify it?
* What has to be done to renovate it?

BASIC STRUCTURE

* *Settlement.* Check entire foundation for settlement which can distort openings, loosen interior finish and siding. Some settlement is not unusual. A few beams or floor joists can be leveled during rehabilitation but numerous failures and general uneven settling may require a new foundation, which would normally preclude rehabilitation.
* *Walls.* Old stone or brick foundations should be checked for cracks and crumbling mortar, which often can be repaired. If extensive, major replacement may be required. Poured concrete walls often have unimportant hairline cracks; however, wider open cracks may get worse. Also check interior masonry foundation walls or piers for defects.
* *Damp basements.* Try to check basement a few hours after a heavy rain. There are various causes such as cracks in walls, lack of outside slope *away* from foundation. A high-water table is the one defect usually impossible to correct.
* *Structural frame.* The building frame should be carefully checked for distortion because of foundation failure or improper or inadequate framing (Figure 12-1).
* *Decay damage.* Use a sharp tool to poke and check for soundness of wood members, particularly where wood is close to ground or where exposed to dampness.
* *Termite damage.* There are subterranean termites in non-tropical areas and non-subterranean termites in tropical areas. Subterraneans must get back to their ground or other water source regularly. They do not expose themselves to light and they work within the wood, leaving a sound outside shell. Non-subterraneans do not need direct access to the ground and water and they cut across the wood grain. The subterranean termites work their way up from the ground to the lowest wood members through foundation wall cracks, through wood too close to the soil or through earthen tubes they build on the

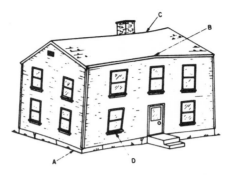

M-142 839

FIGURE 12-1: Uneven foundation settlement: *A*, may result in a house badly out of square. Evidences may include *B*, eaveline distortion; *C*, sagging roof ridge; or *D*, loose-fitting frames or even binding windows.

outside of foundations walls. These tubes are about the thickness of a pencil.
- *Floor post and girders.* Check to make sure that wood floor posts in basement or crawl space are on masonry pedestals rather than embedded in concrete floor. Check girders for sag and for decay where their ends sit in foundation pockets. (See Figure 12-2.)
- *Floor framing.* Similarly, check all floor joists for decay and insect damage and for sag. (See Figure 12-3.) Framing around stairs should be checked carefully for sag.

FIGURE 12-2: Check wood for decay at points of contact with concrete, such as: *A*, floor joists supported on concrete walls; *B*, framing supported in a pocket in a concrete wall; and *C*, wood post supported on a concrete floor.

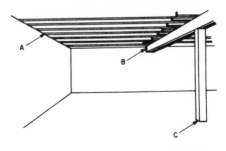

M-143 369

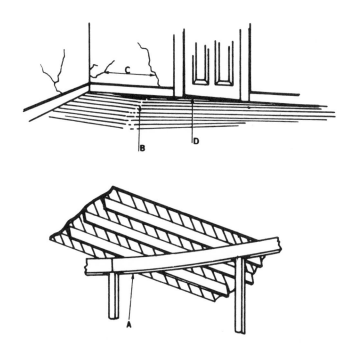

FIGURE 12-3: Badly sagging horizontal member *A*, has resulted in: *B*, uneven floor; *C*, cracked plaster; and *D*, poorly fitting door. (Defects accentuated to illustrate the problems.)

- *Wall framing.* Most walls are strong enough. However, check particularly at the heads of wide window and arch openings for sag in header over openings. New headers may be needed.
- *Roof framing.* Examine the roof for ridge, rafter and/or sheathing sag. (See Figure 12-4.)

NON-STRUCTURAL

- *House exterior.* Building exterior will last a long time if kept free of moisture and given reasonable maintenance. Sometimes expensive re-siding is less expensive than complete removal of peeling paint. However, moisture problems like condensation must first be solved. (See later section.)
- *Siding and trim.* If siding is not badly warped, renailing may rectify. Check siding for decay at butt joints, around window and door frames. Weathered, broken, warped, upturned shingles must be re-sided. Brick or stone veneer cracks can be grouted and joints re-pointed but numerous large or settlement-type cracks may remain very unsightly. Inspect flashing and caulking at all trim, copings, sills and intersections of roofs and walls.

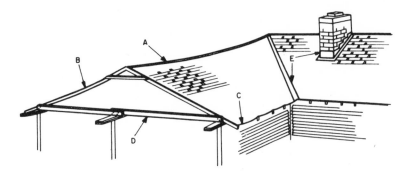

M-143 370

FIGURE 12-4: Watch for sag at *A,* ridge; *B,* rafters; or *C,* sheathing. Rafters are frequently tied, as at ceiling joist, *D,* to prevent them from spreading outward. Flashing, *E,* is used at intersections of two roofs or between roof and vertical planes.

- *Roof.* Roof or flashing leaks become obvious upon inspection of ceilings. Most asphalt shingles last no longer than 20 years; wood roofs up to 30 years. Bubbles or blisters on flat roofs generally indicate need for major repairs. Houses without roof overhangs cause additional maintenance on siding and window trim.
- *Windows, doors, porches.* If the windows are not standard and double-glazed, rehabilitation will be more expensive. Check bottoms of all exterior doors. Check all porch posts, steps near the ground for decay and insect damage.
- *Chimneys, fireplaces.* Look for cracks, loose mortar. See that chimney flue does not touch wood. Check fireplace damper and draft.

HOUSE INTERIOR

- *Flooring, walls.* Excessive layers of wallpaper or very thick, "alligatored" paint are difficult to remove and may have to be covered with panelling. Check condition of wood floor; sanding may restore it.
- *Trim, cabinets.* Match existing, damaged trim or cabinets.
- *Insulation, moisture control.* In view of today's high energy costs, insulation is a must in rehabilitation. Yet, if you add insulation to interior wall spaces without installing an effective vapor barrier or in attics without adequate ventilation, you may ruin a good old house quickly because of condensation problems created in the walls and in the attic. Vapor barriers should be applied on the warm side of the walls. Effective, large-enough louvers or other vents must be in place in the attic whenever insulation is installed. (See Figure 12-5.)

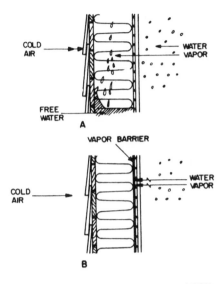

FIGURE 12-5: Vapor barriers reduce moisture problems in walls. *A:* Without a vapor barrier water vapor from the room moves through the wall, is cooled, condenses, and wets the insulation. *B:* Vapor barrier has greatly retarded moisture movement into the walls.

- *Heating, plumbing, electrical.* Check for adequate water pressure, drainage, modern electric service size, branches, outlets and adequate heating plant in good condition. If these mechanical systems have to be replaced, cost will be very high.
- *Layout.* If a dwelling is involved, check to see if kitchen size is adequate, layout efficient, bedroom and bath areas functional and private, room sizes and halls adequate for furniture placement and movement.

13

Tax and Foreclosure Sales: How to Get Your Share of This Hidden Gold Mine

This is where we get into that particularly appropriate little-known profit opportunity for *local* real estate investors, that often secret profit gold mine—tax and foreclosure sales. In this chapter you'll find out how to do business on foreclosures with your friendly local banker. You are also shown how to find your way to big profits through public tax and foreclosure sales and when to stand by for public auctions of foreclosed properties. There is a section on how to read the fine print in newspaper legal notices on these tax and foreclosure sales. The all-important matter of arranging financing for these deals is also covered. Finally there is an appraisal and construction guide for checking out tax and foreclosure sales, *before* bid.

FORECLOSED PROPERTIES FROM BANKS

There are many reasons why properties are forced into sale. Owners default on paying their real estate taxes and/or mortgage payments or both for a variety of reasons. Often it is not only economic pressures. True, many people lose their jobs or go over their heads in debt in our credit culture. They wind up buying so much stuff on credit that there's no money left for taxes or mortgages. Modern life styles and marriage/divorce trends are forcing an ever-increasing number of real estate properties onto the market. There are three divorces nowadays for every five marriages. Many properties are thus thrown suddenly on the resale market and sold through normal channels. Often, however, these domestic discords make it impossible to sell such properties quickly if the real estate market in the area is slow and/or if the separated couple can't even agree long enough to continue tax and mortgage payments while the property is being sold. Death of the owner is another reason for foreclosure of properties in some cases. Marginal small farms which decrease in productivity or where children don't want to continue to farm, are often thrown into foreclosure. Creditors sell off debtors' properties to collect judgments. Commercial properties go out of business. Industrial buildings lose their tenants, etc. A host of factors cause real estate foreclosure sales in our complex society.

LOCAL KNOWLEDGE THE KEY
TO THESE LITTLE-KNOWN DEALS

The trouble with all this continuing, apparently assured supply of properties, many of them at "giveaway" prices, is that much of this supply is usually kept secret. When not deliberate, the very mechanics of this foreclosure sales system, this ancient legal way of transferring properties to collect unpaid debts, operate to restrict public information and access. Required legal notices to owners and the general public are buried in fine print in small newspapers. Often local politicians and others in the know grab up the profitable deals. However, if you understand the system, know where to look, check out the properties to winnow the gold real estate kernels from the chaff, there are fortunes to be made in tax and foreclosure properties.

One great source is your friendly banker. Your secret weapon in this secret foreclosure business is your own knowledge of your area and its properties. You can apply this knowledge directly by talking to the mortgage department of your local bank. Let them know that you may be interested in purchasing properties they are foreclosing. You see, banks are in the mortgage lending business, not in property management. Their bank regulations encourage them to divest themselves of defaulted properties promptly. You can ask to be notified when their properties are going to be auctioned. You can also ask if they have any properties that have already been auctioned and where the bank was the only bidder and took ownership to protect the amount of their mortgages. If they own the property already, you may be able to negotiate a better price with them. Remember, they don't want to continue to own it. They may even agree to offer you a new mortgage to make such a sale feasible so you can buy it and they can get it off their books.

> *Caution:* The fact that the bank is selling the property at or after foreclosure doesn't necessarily mean that it's a good buy. The mortgage might have been too high originally. Be certain to properly appraise for current value of the property before you make your offer.

HOW TO FIND YOUR WAY
TO BIG PROFITS THROUGH FORECLOSURES

People have made fortunes in public tax and other foreclosure sales. A young apartment renter in a western city was recently not given back his $50 "cleaning" deposit when he vacated his apartment even though there was no objection by the owner as to how clean he had left his apartment. This is hard to believe—but he now *owns* this $1.5 million dollar apartment complex where he lived because he was not paid that $50!

This is how his tidy profit happened. It came about specifically because of the mechanics of our ancient legal foreclosure system. When he was refused the $50 repayment, he filed suit in Small Claims Court and won a judgment for $50 plus costs and $200 in damages. The apartment owners paid no attention to his summons and so this 24-year-old creditor requested an execution of sale of the property by the county marshal's office. Only he and the marshal showed up on the county courthouse steps for the "auction." He bid the property in for $450, the amount of his judgment plus additional marshal's fees and interest. He got a marshal's certificate of sale of real estate. The former apartment owner-corporation had a year to redeem the property by paying the $450 (plus interest) but it returned the notice of marshal's sale, unopened. Later, when the corporation tried to sell the apartment complex, the title search turned up the new ownership. This young man was then offered $1000 to clear the title, which he refused, then $10,000, which he also refused. So the corporation filed suit to extend the redemption period on the basis that his acquisition was an "extraordinary windfall." It was!

This bizarre example of rags to riches in foreclosure illustrates the point that specific local knowledge and dogged determination to find one's way through arcane, often complex procedures pay off. Too often in real estate foreclosures, the people in the know, the county clerk personnel and others, learn of foreclosed investment opportunities that are usually beyond the scope of the general public's knowledge. This generally secret world of tax and foreclosure sales, however, has to be *legally* open to the public at various times. This is when the knowledgeable, informed investor can jump in. This is also what you have to know. First, you have to find out where to look for such properties. The following source list identifies many such places to check for the acquiring of tax, foreclosure and government surplus properties:

A FINDER'S LIST OF FORECLOSURE PROPERTIES

1. *Banks.* Although savings and loan institutions are the type of banks that deal mainly in mortgages and delinquent foreclosures, savings, commercial banks and mortgage companies can also be contacted.

2. *Newspaper legal notices.* These required legal notices usually run regularly in local papers and are required reading for investors.

3. *Real estate and property management brokers.* Government agencies like the VA often designate brokers to help sell their foreclosed properties. These brokers have lists available of such properties.

4. *Attorneys.* Local attorneys, particularly those who specialize in real estate, often have information on impending foreclosures.

5. *County clerks.* These offices maintain data on pending sales.

6. *Sheriff, marshal offices.* These offices also maintain such lists.

7. *Newspaper ads.* Many cities and communities insert paid regular newspaper ads to announce annual, semi-annual or special auctions of groups of municipally foreclosed and owned properties.

8. *Title companies.* Local offices of title companies often have such data.

9. *Federal government agencies.* Various agencies have lists of available government-owned surplus and foreclosed property. The *U.S. Department of the Interior,* Bureau of Land Management, has offices from which you can obtain information on public land for sale. These offices are in Anchorage, Phoenix, Sacramento, Reno, Boise, Billings, Santa Fe, Portland (Oregon), Cheyenne, Salt Lake City, as well as the main eastern office at 7981 Eastern Ave., Silver Spring, Md. The *General Services Administration,* Washington, D.C., through its regional offices in New York City, Washington, D.C., Atlanta, Chicago, Fort Worth, Houston, Denver, Los Angeles, San Francisco, and Seattle disposes of surplus federal real estate. (A GSA sale of a former naval reserve center is shown in Figure 13-1.) The *U.S. Department of Housing and Urban Development* (HUD), disposes of dwellings it has foreclosed through its urban homesteading and other programs. (See HUD regional offices list in Chapter 11.) The Department of Agriculture, *Farmers Home Administration* (FmHA), has hundreds of offices in most county seats which help sell their foreclosed rural properties. *The*

FOR

SALE

GOVERNMENT REAL PROPERTY

NAME OF PROPERTY FORMER NAVAL RESERVE CENTER

LOCATION EAST SIDE OF RIVER ROAD,
NEW WINDSOR, NEW YORK

CONSISTING OF APPROXIMATELY 1.4 ACRES OF LAND IN FEE TOGETHER WITH
EASEMENTS FOR ADDITIONAL ACCESS AND UTILITIES --
IMPROVED WITH A QUONSET HUT, A GARAGE, A STORAGE
BUILDING, AND MISCELLANEOUS IMPROVEMENTS.

AS DESCRIBED IN THE ATTACHED INVITATION FOR BIDS NO. GS-02-DRE-91107

SEALED BIDS WILL BE OPENED

DATE
June 6, 1979

TIME
2:00 P.M. LOCAL TIME, NEW YORK, NEW YORK

LOCATION

BUSINESS SERVICE CENTER, BID OPENING ROOM, (ROOM 113)
26 FEDERAL PLAZA, NEW YORK, NEW YORK 10007

GENERAL SERVICES ADMINISTRATION REGION 2, FEDERAL PROPERTY RESOURCES SERVICE,
REAL PROPERTY DIVISION, 26 FEDERAL PLAZA, NEW YORK, NEW YORK 10007

TEL: AREA CODE 212-264-2608

GSA FORM **1740** (REV.

FIGURE 13-1

Veterans Administration (VA) also sells foreclosed properties through its regional offices and designated real estate brokers.

10. *State government agencies.* Various agencies have lists of available state-owned surplus land. Figure 13-2 shows a state brochure ad for 57 acres with buildings and all utilities, estimated value $134,000.

Schoharie County

DESCRIPTION	LOCATION	APPROXIMATE SIZE
Improved, rolling land with 1200 ± ft. on State Rte. 145. One 2-story brick domitory building, one 2-story wooden garage, and one wooden barn.	Town of Middleburg West side on State Rte. 145.	57 Acres

ZONING	UTILITIES	ESTIMATED VALUE
None	All	$134,000

REMARKS

FIGURE 13-2

HOW TO READ THE FINE PRINT
AND STAND BY FOR FORECLOSURE AUCTIONS

Do you want to own a small farm cheap? Do you want to buy a property in the business heart of New York City or in other urban neighborhoods for practically nothing? All this is possible if you regularly study and follow up the sources for such properties in the locality you have chosen. High profits, sometimes fantastic profits, are also possible if you not only go after these "secret" tax and foreclosure deals but also systematically follow the location and checklist step-by-step procedures set down here.

HOW TO PICK UP BACK-TAX
SMALL FARMS CHEAP

Say you want a small farm or farms. Such farmette back-tax bargains are all over the country, many for as little as $25 an acre. I've seen such farms in New York and Pennsylvania go for even less per acre, some even with habitable farm buildings still on them. How do you go about buying such small farms? In some areas, you have to beat the local politicos and even the municipal officers to the best deals, but in many rural areas such sales are open, if not too well advertised. Local newspapers carry notices of such groups of property auctions, usually on a regular basis each year. These properties are usually auctioned off in most states with the minimum "upset" bid being the amount of the unpaid taxes due. In many areas, if no one bids enough, then there is a second sale, with much lower minimum bids and sometimes even negotiated sales on individual parcels. In most states, the owner and/or mortgagee has one to three years to redeem the property by paying back the amount bid plus interest. If no redemption, you get a deed to the property and own it, whether you bid one dollar successfully for the property or many thousands.

HOW TO BUY A PIECE OF THE BIG CITY

Or say you love New York and want to buy a piece of Manhattan. You write to the City of New York Division of Real Property, 1 Police Plaza, N.Y.C., for their current brochure on surplus city-owned real estate. You check out the properties in advance of the listed auction date (see later foreclosure and inspection guide), and after you hold up your hand or finger your right ear, or otherwise win the auction bid, you are given title to a property. It could be a corner building for $13,500 which should make your fortune some day if you are right in your judgment that this is a turnaround area. New York City requirements on down payments at these auctions are fairly typical. For such sales, the successful bidder must have in cash, certified check, bank teller's check, or postal money order, the $13,500 amount required. In addition, if the purchase price is in excess of the minimum upset (lowest acceptable bid) price, an additional deposit, which can be by personal check, is required to be paid on the day of sale.

New York City property auction ground rules are as follows and are similar to those held in other large cities:

- Title reverts to city in two years if housing violations of record are not cleared.
- Purchasers must not own other property tax delinquent over a year.
- Balance of purchase price must be paid and any title objections noted within 30 days of sale.
- Purchasers are advised to check out properties *before* date of sale as to exact location, physical condition, legal use, assessed valuation and annual taxes. (This is good advice in any type of foreclosure or other real estate deal.)

There is very fine print in legal ads which lawyers are required to place in local newspapers, usually several times when they are representing mortgages or other creditors foreclosing on property. These ads give the legal deed (location) description of the property being foreclosed and the date and time when it will be auctioned off on the steps of the county center or town hall. These legal ads are what you have to read carefully. You then check out the properties physically before you stand by the auction steps on that data, down payment handy, ready to bid if you want to invest in such foreclosed properties.

HOW TO ARRANGE FINANCING FOR THESE ALL-CASH DEALS

The financing of tax and foreclosure sales is no different basically than any other kind of real estate investment. Leverage operates in these profit opportunities, as in all real estate investment, to use money of others to pyramid your profits. There are several special points here, however, which have to be understood and stressed:

KEY FINANCING FACTORS IN FORECLOSURES

1. *Cash.* The institutional seller, the county, the bank, the federal government agency or the local sheriff or marshal is, for the most part, interested only in *cash* sales.

2. *Exceptions.* There are a few exceptions to the above general statement. Some federal agencies grant mortgages to buyers on some of their sales. Banks will sometimes make new mortgage commitments to help along the sale of their own foreclosed properties. (Discussed later in this section.)

3. *Deposit.* This cash sale requirement is usually modified on all such public sales only to the extent that a 10% to 20% down payment binds the successful auction bid for about 30 days, after which the balance of the total price is required to be paid in cash or certified check.

4. *Time.* In most tax and foreclosure cases, this cash requirement is needed quickly. It makes it more difficult to get mortgage commitments in time to meet these obligations. Also, since you don't know how much the price of the property is until your final auction bid is accepted, this puts even more stress on the time needed to get maximum financing.

All of these special tax and foreclosure financing factors can be taken into account and handled if you know all the local and other financing sources you can tap. Also, you often have to move more quickly on these types of investments to nail down the mortgage commitment. Chapter 4 lists all financing sources. The following zeroes in on those special lending sources which can be used for tax and foreclosure sales:

SUCCESSFUL WAYS TO GET FORECLOSURE FINANCING

• *Conventional mortgages from institutions.* You can go to savings banks, commercial banks, savings and loan institutions, title and trust companies, building and loan associations and mortgage bankers. For such conventional mortgages, you usually first have to use your own money or short-term financing to meet the time deadline on tax and foreclosure sales. As soon as you are given ownership, you can then *refinance* with long-term, lower-payment mortgages from these conventional sources. It is important, however, that you try to get a *commitment* for such conventional mortgage before you take title to the property.

• *Other financing.* If a bank or mortgage lender is selling a foreclosed property, they are frequently interested in giving you a new loan on the property in order to make the deal possible.

• *Government financing.* The V.A., F.H.A., FmHA all grant direct low-down payment mortgages on practically all the foreclosed properties they sell. (You don't have to be a veteran to get such a mortgage from the V.A. You just have to meet the downpayment and credit requirements.)

• *Additional financing.* Second mortgages from lending companies and individuals to further reduce your cash requirement can be secured, particularly if you have gotten a good buy and the foreclosed property you now own is good collateral.

APPRAISAL-CONSTRUCTION GUIDE
FOR FORECLOSING PROPERTIES

It is an axiom in real estate that you have to get there first to make the most profits. This is particularly true in tax and foreclosure sales. Not only does your auction bid have to be the successful one, but in addition, you usually don't have much time. So it's even more important in these types of investments to touch every value and construction base beforehand. True, you might have to run these tax and foreclosure sale bases more quickly. However, you can't afford to skip any. The following construction and valuation guide is particularly pertinent to tax and foreclosure sales. It specifically supplements the basic land/construction inspection checklist and appraisal guide in Chapter 5:

FORECLOSURE CHECKLIST

LOCATION

• Are community facilities available? Transportation road network or public transportation nearby?
• Rehabilitation signs in area? Any buildings being upgraded? Other turnaround signs?
• Employment in area? Economic conditions?
• Popular area? Active real estate market?

THE LAND

• Block and lot drainage okay?
• No adverse neighbors like junkyards, odors, etc.?
• Public, maintained access road?
• Zoning permits current or contemplated usage?

- Is exterior condition of roof, windows, doors, siding, other exterior improvements, etc., acceptable?
- Is interior condition safe, sanitary, structurally acceptable, or have neglect and vandalism due to vacancy caused damage unfeasible to correct?

INSPECTION CAUTIONS

- Inspection must be objective. One's natural adverse reaction to the usual neglect and abuse of such properties by former defaulted owners and others must not blind the inspector.
- Look for basic location, turnaround and sound structural factors to determine whether the property is feasible for purchase and repair.

VALUATION

- *The price must be right.* In valuation analysis of tax and foreclosure properties, as in all real estate investment, you can hire professional appraisers but your local knowledge of the deal, your total analysis and your decision on the price you bid must be yours alone.
- *Valuation* must be in two parts. You have to come up with an *as-is* value which you will bid at or under, and an *as-rehabilitated* value which you can anticipate when the property is brought back to full, usable and marketable condition.
- *Cost of repairs.* The potential value is not merely the total of as-is value plus cost of repairs. You still need a good cost estimate on the amount of money that will be the absolute bottom line below which you can lose, not make money.
- *Market approach.* (See Chapter 5 on how to appraise using the market approach.) This approach is the best way to value tax and foreclosure properties. However, as previously stated, you have to come up with *two* values. The best way is to use two sets of comparables, one for as-is value and one for as-rehabilitated value. For example, say you are interested in bidding on a vacant two-family dwelling which has had a freeze-up and needs considerable heating, plumbing and interior finish repair. It's in a fair urban neighborhood which shows signs of getting much better because young executives are moving in. You study the overall region, the area, the real estate market and at least three recent comparable sales of similar properties, similarly situated. You adjust for differences and come up with your best estimate of as-rehabilitated value. Then you determine the cost of the needed repairs. However, as stated before, you don't just deduct the cost of repairs, which you have to know, for cash flow purposes. In all such successful deals, upgrading the property will put more value on the property than just the cost of repairs added. If you can find another set of comparable sales in similar location and *rundown* condition, that's the best way to get as-is value. If not, then deduct the cost of

repairs, overhead and anticipated profit from the as-rehabilitated value and also deduct a contingency-valuation factor of at least 50% more (of the total repairs amount) to come up with your maximum bid price.

- *Income approach.* (See also Chapter 5.) This approach is used only on commercial properties and then only when comparable sales for a market approach cannot be found. The cost approach should not be used on tax and foreclosure sales.
- *Valuation caution.* As in construction inspections, it is important that you or the appraiser don't ascribe the sins of its former owners to the property itself. Look beyond the neglect, dirt and rundown condition for basic value when it's cleaned up. If it's sound and if similar sales of upgraded properties in the area justify purchase, objectivity is the path to profits. If you can get it for less or much less at the auction because competitive bidders haven't done their homework and been as objective, that too is the name of this profit game in tax and foreclosure properties.

14

Timber, Riparian, Air and Mineral Rights: How to Make These Big Spinoff Profits

This chapter is on those especially little-known, unique ways to make money in real estate—the buying and selling of easement and other property rights. The first section covers sale of timber rights. Other sections deal with riparian water rights, mineral rights, development rights, oil, gas and other rights including how you find, buy and sell them for big profits.

A PROFITS ANALYSIS OF RIGHTS

All these rights stem from ancient legal definitions of land ownership. When you buy a piece of land, you buy it in "fee simple" most of the time, which means that you are buying all the rights that go with the property except those belonging to the state (police, eminent domain, escheat and taxation). These property rights are called the "bundle of rights." When you own your land parcel within its legally described boundary lines, you also own all the ground below the surface and all the air above the land. That's what this chapter is all about. You not only can profit from the sale of your land or subdivided portions of your land; you can also sell or rent part of the "bundle of rights" you bought. It can be the ground surface or the minerals below or the air above. It can be the timber that grows on it or your development rights or the water that it adjoins or is under. By sale of such rights (or lease), you are diminishing your bundle of rights. However, this is one real estate area where you can take your cake of profits for one or more of the rights and still have and own the land and the balance of your rights.

PROFITING FROM TIMBER RIGHTS
WITHOUT ECOLOGICAL DAMAGE

More than half the softwood timber the nation needs for its building is now in national forests. The lumber companies are cutting trees on their own lands faster than they can be replaced. The demand for lumber as well as its price continues to increase. At the same time, public demand for recreational use of these forests is increasing. Government regulation of these forests in terms of timber cutting is reflecting this mounting interest in recreational use. More and more millions of acres of forestland are being restricted against timber cutting.

Yet there are still vast areas, as in New England, where forests are growing wood twice as fast as it is being removed. Recent studies show that more than 80% of New England is now forested again, up from 20% a hundred years ago when the land was almost fully cleared. The land there is also now in small acreage parcels, averaging ten-acre plots. Rising prices of oil and gas have made the price of firewood jump to over $100 a cord, particularly close to urban areas. In this New England area, owners of even these small tracts can sell off timber rights because the price has become right. In the Northeast, these reforested areas have much wood that is made up of "inferior" trees, stumps and sprouts, struggling for a share of water, nutrients and light. Sale of logging rights can be a useful tool to supplement nature's own culling management and help to reduce natural disasters like fire. Sale of timber rights also pays off in cash.

Examples of Profits from Timber Rights

On one ten-acre tract in a small Northeast town recently, we sold 10,369 board feet of tulip trees, 802 board feet of maple and 2358 board feet of red oak. The logger paid us $3150. Another 21-acre wood lot with better trees yielded $6200. Both parcels are still heavily wooded; no erosion or other ecological damage has resulted and we still own the land. There are also lanes now that will help fight forest fires.

In Ohio recently, a black walnut tree with a 57-foot-long, 48-inch wide trunk sold for $30,000! A 250-acre farm with heavily wooded sections in that same state yielded $76,000 in timber rights *before* it was developed and sold off in large acreage lots.

MAKING AN EASY PROFIT AND TAX BREAK THROUGH SOUND TIMBER MANAGEMENT

The sale of timber rights, carefully managed, is very profitable. It is also very simple to sell these rights nowadays. There is such a strong, continuing demand for soft and hard woods that buyers will generally beat paths to landowners' doors.

Money can be saved as well as made in proper forest management. Many communities encourage forests on land tracts by offering substantial property tax exemptions to property owners who practice forest conservation. Contact your local tax assessor for information on such tax exemptions.

GUIDELINES FOR SALE OF TIMBER RIGHTS

However, the landowner must be on guard against property damage and fraud. You can hire a forestry consultant from lists provided by the Association of Consulting Foresters, Box 369, Yorktown, Virginia 23690.

Here are some basic guidelines:

- Proper logging can create cross-country skiing, jeep and fire lanes.
- It can free growing space for the best young trees.
- Greatest damage from logging operation on steep slopes is erosion from trucks and machinery. Logging roads have to be put in carefully.
- Skidding, the dragging of trees, also causes erosion. Crawler-tractors are lighter on the land than rubber-tired skidders. Skidding on frozen or dry ground also causes less damage.
- Logging contracts should spell out how the roads, particularly on slopes, will be protected when logging is finished. They should be seeded. Water-bars, angled earth piles topped with gravel, should also be installed to deflect water.

LAKESIDE GORES AND RIPARIAN LAND

As first shown in Chapter 6, "gore" is defined as "a piece of land, generally small, irregular, odd-shaped, triangular or tapering." Gores often result when a new road bisects a parcel of land. When the gore is located alongside a body of water, it often becomes valuable even though it may be tiny and not, or barely, developable.

A lake gore is given value because of its location on or even in a body of water. "Riparian" is defined as "pertaining to, or being on, the bank of a river, of a lake or of a tidewater." What gives the gore its value in such riparian locations is that most people yearn for access to water. You don't need much dry land to park a boat trailer. Once launched, you can boat, sail or fish the entire lake even though you have legal entry only from a tiny gore.

How a Doctor Bought onto a One-Mile Lake for $2,000

A local doctor I know bought such a lakeside gore on a small lake recently. This tiny, irregular 30' × 45' gore even had an existing small boathouse on it. He paid less than $2000 for the parcel. He's been offered many thousands more for it but prefers to continue to sail his boat out of the boathouse and relax on his float anchored 30 feet off his gore. Chapter 6 details procedures for locating and buying such small dots of land surrounding many lakes because roads usually run close to the lake edges. Ownership can be traced easily through assessor office records.

There is a large demand for *ownership* of such riparian parcels on bodies of water. There is an equally big market for *easement rights* to water. Many land deed descriptions still contain old reservations for access to lakes and streams established when the parcels were sold in the past. These reservations or rights usually went to the sellers and their *assigns*. Assigns are legally those persons to whom the sellers or their heirs later give or sell their rights. So, given this yearning for water-oriented recreation, here is another very special, very profitable, little-known real estate step-by-step procedure to make money, through local knowledge and contacts:

KEY STEPS TO LAKE RIGHTS

Step 1. Locate the body of water. Study the lake, stream or tidewater. Are there government controls such as reservoir uses which prohibit most recreation uses? If existing recreational usages indicate no restrictions and if there are no new controls, then go on to the next step.

Step 2. Visit the county record office. Research all the waterfront parcels thoroughly. You can pay for this service by hiring a title company to give you a report or you can do the following research yourself.

Step 3. Study the tax map. Most communities now have tax maps which show the property lines of all properties in the community. Copy down all the tax section, block and lot numbers for each waterfront parcel. Then review the tax roll which lists all these plots and gives the owners' names.

Step 4. Review all the land deeds. Using the names from Step 3, identify each deed liber (book) and page number from the county clerk's alphabetical deed index book. Then you can quickly skim through each deed, looking only for deeded easement rights. Copy down the names of the rights' holders for each deed.

Step 5. Contact the rights' holders. This is where local knowledge really can be useful. In old deeds, you may have to contact heirs. Newspaper libraries can be used to trace current locations of heirs. In any event, if you researched enough of the deeds, you're bound to find some, and each one is potentially very profitable.

Step 6. Buy the rights. Buy it for use, for resale or for later sale for higher profits.

Step 7. Use or sell the rights. Once you find and buy or option such lake rights, you can enjoy their use yourself or sell them to others. Such sales of these desirable rights are readily made through the usual real estate channels of brokers, local and area newspaper advertising.

How One Site's Cut Became Another's Fill

Sometimes in real estate development for profits, you don't have to sell the rights to others to take out the sand or gravel or other soil or aggregates from the site you own or plan to buy. You can do it yourself. Chapter 2 details how one enterprising investor cut down large shale banks on his bowling alley property to the parking lot level. He trucked this shale to fill up a lot he had bought cheaply for just this cut-and-fill procedure. The lot he bought was very low. The shale fill that he moved to his low site made it level to the road. Now he has doubled the parking for his bowling alley. He also sold the filled lot to a fast-food pizza chain for tens of thousands of dollars of net profit—after deducting the cost of purchase, excavation and trucking.

A development I appraised had received approval for a Planned Unit Development of homes and a shopping center. The site had an excellent location next to the ramp of an interstate highway. The trouble was that it was low and needed an average three feet of fill on half of the 63 acres. Purchase of fill by the yard would have made the whole project unfeasible. So the developer looked around and found and bought a 25-acre tract nearby with a small hill on it. He moved most of the hill to his P.U.D. site. Now he has not one but two developable sites.

PROFITING FROM AIR RIGHTS

Besides surface rights like timber, soil and right-of-way easement access rights to water, there are also air rights in property ownership. This is the owner's right to all the air above his land contained within his property lines. Recently, such air rights have become valuable and are being bought and sold, particularly in denser urban areas.

New York City was the forerunner in encouraging and profiting from sale of air rights. Its laws permit sale or lease of air space above proposed schools to developers who pay the city an annual sum instead of real estate taxes. The city has even leased air space above public buildings to developers of adjoining properties.

PROFITABLE USES OF AIR RIGHTS

This profitable use of rights to air space is beginning to happen now not only in cities but also at high-density or high-traffic locations in suburban and even in rural areas. Such air space development has included the following uses:

- Office buildings over parking garages.
- Apartment houses over highways.
- Manufacturing buildings over streets.
- Hospitals over streets.
- Buildings over schools.
- Shopping centers over railroad tracks.

Other modern uses could be:

- Motels over highway interchanges.
- Marinas over *non-navigable* waters like lakes and waterways. (The federal government through its condemnation laws can take away any construction over navigable waters without compensation.)

When you buy or sell air rights, the special features of tax allocation, building column location and maintenance have to be considered carefully. How much does the surface ownership pay in taxes compared to the air rights? Where do you put the columns for the air space improvements for minimum interference with surface improvements?

MINERAL, GRAVEL, OIL, GAS
AND OTHER PROFITABLE RIGHTS

Whether on the ground, above the ground or underground, property rights without ownership, at different times and in different areas, have different values—sometimes spectacularly high values. If you know your local area, have your finger on the pulse of its economy, and know the real estate market, you're in the best position to make big profits from buying and selling any or all of the following property rights:

PROFITS FROM SUBSURFACE
SAND AND GRAVEL

Sand and gravel "borrow pits," shale banks and rock blasted into small traprock pieces have been the basic building material for suburban expansion. These construction material aggregates are needed for concrete and masonry products, for paving our roads and building our buildings.

Since WWII, these borrow pits have soared in value, depending on location, grade of material, available supply and distance to construction going on in the area. In 20 years, I have witnessed bulk sand and gravel go up in price in my own county from 25¢ a yard, "run of the bank," truck-it-yourself, to $4. Many of these pits contained a million yards or more. Recently a local airport was approved for major concrete runway extension. Excavation rights at even higher prices were immediately bought up on every piece of land in the area that had good deposits and a permit for excavation. Now, contractors in the area who need construction aggregates can't find any local materials. They have to buy expensive traprock, processed miles downriver and barged to this area at high cost. One of the borrow pits taken for the airport was bought less than ten years ago for $1100 an acre for 35 acres. Subsurface contour surveys revealed 150,000 available yards of good material. This landowner paid $38,500. He sold the rights for $60,000. A tidy profit—and he still owns the land.

When purchasing land or selling the rights to land with subsurface deposits of such materials, you should secure drilling reports, spotted throughout the acreage so that a subsurface contour survey may be plotted together with the surveyor's estimate of number of yards of material. You should make certain the land already has an excavation permit or is zoned by right for such mining. You can use the subsurface survey later to resurvey and to measure the charge by the yard excavated, if that's how the contract on the sale of the rights for excavation is set up. Also, you should specify in your contract with the excavator basic land reclamation requirements such as re-seeding, proper slope grading and reforesting as necessary.

OIL, GAS RIGHTS

In today's desperate energy times, exploration for oil and gas deposits is going into many new areas. Although comparatively small exploration lease rents are paid, usually only about $2 per acre per year, there is the industry's standard royalty of 12.5% if a commercially producing reserve is found.

This is how you get in on the royalty profits from these gas and oil rights on government land. The Department of Interior sells non-competitive oil and gas leases, mainly in the western states where most of the public land is located. A few tracts in the Midwest and East are also sometimes leased. These leases are made through non-competitive drawings by lottery. Tract sizes range from under 40 acres to a maximum of 2560 acres. There is a $10 filing fee and annual rental fees of $1 per acre for the exclusive rights to explore for and remove oil and gas. No surface rights are conveyed other than these oil and gas development rights. The values of these leases vary. If they are in "hot" areas near known oil and gas developed land, profits can average several dollars or more per acre if you resell (assign) your rights to a drilling company. Many investors use a filing service which, for a fee, evaluates the more desirable sites and does the actual filings. The Department of Interior, however, cautions that investors do not have to use such services. You can do it yourself. Additional information, free entry cards and the specific cost of monthly lists of land available for leasing many be obtained from the Bureau of Land Management offices listed on the next page.

Development Rights. Sometimes you can make money from selling rights to *do nothing* on your property—or at least nothing more than you have been doing. For example, in Nassau County, New York, and Kings County, State of Washington, these two mainly suburbanized counties have enabling laws which permit them to buy up the development rights on thousands of acres of farmland. In Kings County, dairy, berry and vegetable farmers faced high property taxes and increasing pressure to sell their land to housing and industrial developers. In Nassau County, potato and vegetable farmers were

STATE OFFICES
U.S. DEPARTMENT OF INTERIOR
BUREAU OF LAND MANAGEMENT

Arizona:
2400 Valley Bank Center
Phoenix, AZ 85073

California:
Federal Bldg.
2800 Cottage Way
Sacramento, CA 95825

Colorado:
Colorado State Bank Bldg.
1600 Broadway
Denver, CO 80202

Idaho
Federal Bldg.
550 West Fort St.
P.O. Box 042
Boise, ID 83724

Montana, N. Dakota and S. Dakota
222 N. 32 St., PO Box 30157
Billings, MT 59107

Nevada
Federal Bldg., 300 Booth St.
Reno, NV 89509

New Mexico, Okla. and Texas
US Post Office & Federal Bldg.
PO Box 1449
Santa Fe, NM 87501

Oregon and Washington
729 N.E. Oregon St., PO Box 2965
Portland, OR 97208

Utah
Univ. Club Bldg., 136 E. South Temple
Salt Lake City, UT 84111

Wyoming, Kansas and Nebraska
2515 Warren Av., PO Box 1828
Cheyenne, WY 82001

*States East of Mississippi & Iowa,
Minn., Missouri, Ark. & Louisiana*
Eastern States Office,
7891 Eastern Av.,
Silver Spring, MD 20910

beset by the same economic problems. Agricultural exemptions on taxes helped but did not resolve the situation. So the counties actually purchased development rights from the farmers and other non-farming owners of vacant tracts. Under the plan, land is assessed at two levels—value as agricultural land and value to a potential developer. Owners who accept the county offers receive the difference. For example, if you own 30 acres assessed at $1000 an acre as farmland and worth $10,000 for its "highest and best use" as a development, you would receive $9000 times 30 or $270,000. You could then use your land only for farming or leave it open as fallow land so long as it is not developed.

Abandoned Railroad Rights-of-Way. Chapter 6 details an example of one investor who bought and profited from a two-mile long 50-long wide strip of land abandoned by a railroad no longer operating. There are more and more railroad rights-of-way being abandoned in America today. Real estate is dynamic. You can buy up such R.O.W.'s in long strips, then sell them back at big profits to the heirs (and assigns) of the property owners who had sold the R.O.W. to the railroad over a hundred years ago in the first place. History repeats itself.

Recent Amtrack railroad line cutbacks involve abandoning thousands of miles of tracks and service. The Interstate Commerce Commission, Washington, D.C. 20423 (202-254-6550) can answer questions on this abandonment application process.

Miscellaneous Property Rights. There are various other little-known ways to profit from buying and selling property rights if you use your local knowledge and this guidance. There are *scenic easements* where the easement buyer, government or private, pays you *not* to erect on certain areas of your land signs or other structures that will block scenic views. There are *pipeline* easements where utility transmission companies buy the right to run their gas or other pipelines under your land. There are *road access easements* where public or private easement buyers purchase the right to cross your land and pave the resulting right-of-way. There are *flowage* easements, usually involved in condemnation cases, where a public body buys the right to cover your land with water for a dam or to raise a reservoir's height or to create a recreational lake. There are *aviation* rights where property owners sell their right to build or grow trees above a certain height to prevent destruction of low-flying planes. There are even *temporary* easement rights like slope and working easements alongside new or widened roads.

A SUMMARY BLUEPRINT FOR RIGHTS PROFITS

In sum, this little-known real estate field of rights is very profitable. You can own, buy and sell these rights through customary real estate channels the same as the land that gives off these rights. Again, what you have to do to profit from these little-known rights is use your local knowledge and contacts and apply the guidelines given here.

15

Historical Properties: How to Get Big Profits and Tax Savings from These Real Estate Profit Opportunities

This is an especially important chapter devoted to that little-known new phenomenon—rehabilitation of historic properties. Recent federal and state historical preservation laws are shown here to have opened a whole new income tax and real estate profit bonanza. A section of this chapter shows how these new laws not only encourage historical renovation profits but also penalize heavily those property owners who demolish historic properties to rebuild them new. The "secret ingredient" of excellent accelerated depreciation and other income tax incentives for historical rehabilitation are then detailed, including illustrative case studies. Step-by-step procedures are set down, including specimen application forms, for getting in on the profits and tax savings from rehabilitation of historical properties. There are detailed sections on how to profit from rehabilitating in turnaround areas and restoring historic railroad stations. Finally, a summary of these historical property profit opportunities is presented.

RECENTLY ENACTED HISTORICAL
PRESERVATION LAWS:
A TAX AND PROFIT BONANZA

Until very recently, our country grew by expansion and by tearing down old structures to build "bigger and better." This practice contrasted with that of most older nations like England and other countries that protect their national heritages (and their property values) by maintaining and restoring historic properties. In many of our cities, government policies of agencies like Housing and Urban Development had after WWII helped to destroy many fine neighborhoods through their "urban renewal" policies, which mainly wrecked rather than renewed. In the suburbs, fine historic properties were bulldozed aside to make way for roads, houses, shopping centers and industry. In the mid-sixties, "urban pioneers" began to return from the suburbs to the cities where they found cheap buildings, many in old historic districts, which they could rehabilitate for much less than they could buy for in the suburbs. Thus, places like Brooklyn Heights in Brooklyn, N.Y., began to see deterioration slowed in the early sixties. Prior to that time, I had appraised dwellings in that historic district for $10,000 to $15,000. By the seventies, prices were beginning to range from $100,000 to $250,000 for dwellings similar to the one in the photograph shown here.

Although preservation groups had labored to save such historic properties earlier, Section 2124 of the Tax Reform Act of 1976 gave the main impetus to historical preservation throughout our land. It did this by establishing important tax incentives for the preservation of historic commercial and income-producing structures. The U.S. Department of the Interior followed this up with implementing regulations designed to discourage demolition and encourage rehabilitation as well as charitable donation of partial interests such as facade easements in significant historical properties.

Successful Examples of Historical Money-Makers

This is not a small select group of real estate money-makers. We're talking about an estimated potential of 700,000 properties of all types. These include fine old residences of distinctive design and quality finish. Although historical rehabilitation is really just beginning, actual projects have already been successfully started, like factory buildings and waterfront structures in Boston which have been turned into offices and luxury apartments. In Denver, a brewery

was converted into a shopping and entertainment complex. In many cities, whole blocks of formerly dilapidated rooming house neighborhoods are being transformed into fine restored multiple dwelling townhouses. Restaurants, banks and offices are showing particular promise as successful tenants of restored commercial historical properties.

This is happening not only in the Northeast—where Washington slept in so many antique houses—but also in the old and "new" South. It is taking place in the West and even in the comparatively new Far West. Projects are just beginning to exploit this new investment trend and this encouraging tax law throughout our land. Rehabilitation of historic properties is starting everywhere. Thus, high up in the San Bernardino mountains, a California housewife, aided and abetted by her attorney-husband, has applied for historic certification and is restoring one of the first ranches in that region. The early-1900s Hotel Oakland in California will be occupied by new apartments and shops. Even "Art's Auto" was recently added to the Register of Historic Places in Rhode Island. This one-story commercial building, only 14 feet wide by 32 feet long, with roof turrets, was built only 50 years ago, to "stop traffic" on its highway for business purposes by its Coney Island type of architecture. It too is now an official landmark.

So, for properties dating from the American Colonial era to comparatively recent times, up to 50 years ago, federal and state laws now identify historic properties and offer special profits and tax benefits if you protect rather than demolish them.

HOW TO RESTORE, NOT DEMOLISH, FOR BIG PROFITS

Section 2124 of Public Law 94-455, known as the Tax Reform Act of 1976, uses the carrot and stick method to encourage historical preservation—the "carrot" of profit and tax incentives for those who restore and the "stick" of denial of any depreciation at all for those who demolish.

These are most important incentives in real estate investment which is one of the few investment fields left where capital gains and income can still be sheltered. These tax incentives for rehabilitation are major investment considerations and will be fully detailed in later sections. Regarding demolition, the tax penalties are severe for those who demolish historic structures and replace them with new construction.

For example, if you demolish such a certified historic structure, the demolition costs or losses you sustain as a result of the structure's removal must be capitalized. In other words, these costs or losses have to be added to the cost of the land, rather than being currently deductible along with the remaining undepreciated basis of the demolished building. Not only do you lose these deductions, but also the law prohibits accelerated depreciation in whole or in part on new construction erected on a site that was occupied by a certified historic structure.

The law does all this to discourage demolition. However, if the owner of a structure within a registered Historic District receives written certification from the National Park Service prior to demolition that his structure is not of historic significance to its district, then he will not be subject to the demolition penalties. However, the burden, as always, is on the applicant to prove that demolition is warranted. Also recent Supreme Court decisions are beginning to support historic rehabilitation rather than renewal. Thus, the traditional legal approach to appraising properties at their "highest and best use" may be changing to reflect the Supreme Court ruling in the Grand Central Terminal case of "a reasonable return" for a "reasonable use." This new legal approach to valuation of real estate should also support those who restore and rehabilitate rather than demolish and rebuild.

This Historic Preservation Law is being enforced in these punitive aspects. Government agencies like the Veterans Administration require that their appraisers certify on every property appraised whether or not it is in a historical district.

In any event, it is estimated that there will be about 700,000 properties either individually listed or located in and certified to be significant to a district listed in the National Register of Historic Places or in a historic district designated by a state or local authority and certified federally. It is overwhelmingly clear that this public law and accompanying regulations make it much easier to make money by preserving rather than by destroying these investment opportunities.

HOW TO USE CERTIFIED REHABILITATION OF HISTORIC PROPERTIES FOR BIG TAX DEDUCTIONS

On the other hand, the "carrot" of tax incentives for greater profit is made readily available to rehabbers of historic structures in such historic districts. You can cash in high profit and tax dollars by buying and rehabilitating such properties. This is what is involved and how it works:

• *First Step.* The building must be a certified historic structure. To start the ball rolling, contact your State Historic Preservation Officer. (See list of state officers and addresses in Figure 15-2.)
• *Second Step.* Fill out the application for certification. The state

officer has 45 days to review your application and send it with his recommendations to the National Park Service. The whole process should take three or four months. You can be under construction during this time. However, to avoid mistakes which can cost you later tax breaks, you should, if at all possible, send in your application *before* you start.

• *Third Step.* Complete the renovation which must not only be on a structure certified through the above application process but also must involve a commercial, industrial, or residential, rental, depreciable (income-producing) property, with costs incurred before July, 1981.

• *Fourth Step.* Choose either one of the big tax breaks detailed below:

1. *Accelerated depreciation.* If you rehabilitate for *residential rental* use, you can take 200% declining balance depreciation (the same as if it were a new building) instead of the 125% declining balance method used on old residential buildings. If it is for *commercial or industrial* use, you can use the 150% declining balance method (instead of straight line only) using this rapid depreciation in all types of property on *both* the building and the rehabilitation costs. This accelerated depreciation is only for "substantial" rehabilitation, meaning that your rehab costs must exceed what you paid for the property (or $5000 if that's higher).

2. *Five-year write-off.* Even if the rehabilitation is not substantial, you can write off your rehabilitation costs over only five years, rather than the building's longer actual useful life. You still have to write off the building shell over its useful life.

A Specific Example of Big Tax Savings

Say you bought a large old building for $100,000, including $80,000 worth of structure and $20,000 for land. It is certified as historic and you borrow $200,000 to do the rehabilitation into rental apartments. Assume a 25-year life for the building. The bottom-line arithmetic by either Method #1 or Method #2 is as follows:

Method #1. You use 200% declining balance depreciation to write off the $280,000 (building plus rehabilitation). This gives you a $22,400 tax deduction the first year.

Method #2. You can write off the $200,000 (rehab cost) over five years. That's $20,000 in tax deductions *each* year for five years. In addition, using 125% declining balance, you can take a $4000 depreciation deduction on the building shell the first year.

By either method, your depreciation (piled on top of those deductions for mortgage interest, real estate taxes, etc.) can be utilized to offset the rental income from the property. Excess write-off will help shelter your other income from tax. Owners can even take income tax deductions while they await approval of their application for certification subject to collection if not approved. Two additional case study examples prepared by the U.S. Office of Archeology and Historic Preservation (Figure 15-1) illustrate both large and small historic rehabilitation profits and the tax savings and profits that result.

Syndicators active in renovation are buying up old decrepit buildings in historic districts and converting them to subsidized housing and commercial space. The syndicate investors then receive their share of profits and tax savings minus the fees of the syndicator. This is a classic case of the real estate pro going where the new little-known profitable action is. There are plenty of such historic properties to go around, large and small enough for all those who are interested in making high profits and big tax savings.

HOW TO GET IN ON THE HUNDREDS OF THOUSANDS OF HISTORIC PROPERTIES BEING REHABILITATED

To get in on this action in historical properties, you have to own or buy a property that is in or can be in an historical district. It also has to be income producing, industrial, commercial or residential rental. The following ad recently appeared in the real estate section of a Northeast newspaper:

Historical District—Needs major restoration—no money down to qualified sincere individual. Call _____.

This ad demonstrates a seller interested in helping to preserve a historical property by offering attractive terms. Other sources for locating such potential investment properties are of course real estate brokers, local historical societies and most important, as always, your own local knowledge of your own area. You should contact your State Historic Preservation Officer (see Figure 15-2) for up-to-date locations of historic districts in your area. You can also consult the Federal Register in any large library for historical district data. This Register comes out each February with regular monthly updates.

Once you have the property, you have to get it certified and rehabilitated. You file a two-part form, "Historic Preservation Certification Application," with your State Historic Preservation Office, *in duplicate,* to have the Secretary of the Interior determine whether the property is historically significant to the district. If the structure is

The following case studies were prepared by Sarah G. Old-
ham of the Office of Archeology and Historic Preservation,
National Park Service, in consultation with Coopers & Ly-
brand, Certified Public Accountants, to illustrate generally
the incentives and disincentives of the historic preservation
provisions of the Tax Reform Act. The reader should keep in
mind that conclusions concerning the best course of action for
a taxpayer will vary with each person according to his or her
individual financial situation.

The economic feasibility of any potential rehabilitation project depends on numerous factors including
an investor's financial expectations, project location,
requirements for local project review, and timing.
The Tax Reform Act offers certain incentives that
can either tip the balance to convince an investor to
proceed with a rehab project or make an already vi-
able project even more attractive from the financial
point of view. The following are three simplified hypothetical case studies to illustrate the possible effects of the Tax Reform Act historic preservation
provisions.

Mr. Danford, an unmarried accountant who earns
$26,000 a year, decides to buy a residence as rental
property. The house and land, which he purchased in
January 1977 for $30,000 are located in a National
Register historic district. Mr. Danford spends
$35,000 to rehabilitate the exterior of the house and
converts the interior to three rental apartment units,
retaining the small amount of remaining historic interior trim in accordance with the Secretary of the Interior's "Standards for Rehabilitation." Mr. Danford
fills out parts 1 and 2 of the National Park Services'
Tax Reform Act application (the certification of significance within a historic district and certification of
rehabilitation), sends both to his State Historic Preservation Office (SHPO), obtains the necessary certification and proceeds to prepare his 1977 tax return.

The lot on which Mr. Danford's house stands is
worth $10,000. Using the accelerated depreciation
method allowed for "substantial rehabilitation" under the Tax Reform Act, Mr. Danford can depreciate
the $20,000 cost of the house ($30,000 − $10,000)
as well as the $35,000 rehabilitation cost
($20,000 + $35,000 = $55,000, the adjusted basis
of the property) by the 200% declining balance
method applicable to residential rental properties
(depreciation on a commercial property cannot exceed the 150% declining balance method).

Assuming a 25 year life for the property, Mr. Danford can deduct $4,400 from his first year tax return
($55,000 × 1/25 × 200%); because Mr. Danford's
income (salary + net rental income) puts him in a
40% tax bracket, his taxes will be reduced by $1,760
($4,400 × 40%). Under the old law the maximum
first year deduction would have been $2,750
($55,000 × 1/25 × 125%) for a tax savings of
$1,100 ($2,750 × 40%). Not only does Mr. Danford pay several hundred dollars less in taxes thanks
to the Tax Reform Act provisions but also his investment property may bring him income from three
rental units as well as the appreciation on the original
cost of the house and rehabilitation.

1.) Mr. Danford's Rental Property

Acquisition Cost		$30,000
Cost of land		10,000
Cost of house	$55,000 basis for	
depreciation purposes		20,000
Rehabilitation Cost		35,000
First year depreciation 55,000 × 1/25 × 200%		4,400
Reduction in taxes	**4,400 × 40%**	**1,760**

In the foregoing hypothetical case, Mr. Danford
took advantage of the Tax Reform Act's "substantial
rehabilitation" provision. Another example illustrates a larger investor's use of the 60 month amortization provision.

Mrs. Conway, a real estate broker and developer
whose annual income reported jointly with her husband's averages about $150,000, purchased an old
warehouse in a historic district for $130,000 in Janu-
ary 1977. She hired an architect to prepare drawings
to convert the warehouse into an indoor sports facility in accordance with the Secretary of the Interior's
"Standards for Rehabilitation" and at a rehab cost of
$250,000. The architect filled out Sections 1 and 2 of
the Tax Reform Act application, Mrs. Conway signed
the form, and subsequently she obtained the necessary certifications from the Department of the Interi-
or.

Amortizing the rehabilitation expenditures over 5
years, Mrs. Conway is able to deduct $50,000 (one-
fifth of $250,000) the first year from her tax return,
reducing her taxes by $33,000 because the Conways'
income places them in a 66% tax bracket ($50,000 ×
66%). Mrs. Conway also depreciates the original cost
of the warehouse minus the land cost. After 4 years,
Mrs. Conway sells the sports facility for $500,000.

At the end of the year, her tax consultant com-
putes her taxes on the profit from the sale which he
arrives at by deducting the adjusted basis of the property from the sales price (sales price minus original
cost of the warehouse plus rehabilitation expenses
minus amortization deductions already claimed and
depreciation deductions taken on the purchase price
of the warehouse minus land value). Although she
will pay substantially more in taxes on her gross profit than she would have had she depreciated her rehabilitation costs over the life of the building rather
than amortizing them under the Tax Reform Act provision, the reduced taxes due to the amortization will
have allowed her the use of $132,000 ($33,000 × 4
years) for other investment purposes in the interim.

As demonstrated in the expanded case study that
follows this one, her after tax profit, even taking into
account the recapture provision of the Act as origi-
nally passed, will be greater under the amortization
provision of the Tax Reform Act than before its
enactment. Moreover, her project costs may have
been lower than the cost of construction of a new
facility, the construction period may have been short-
er and the consumer attraction value as well as the
resale value of the sports facility may have been increased by its historical character.

2.) Mrs. Conway's Sports Facility

Acquisition Cost		$130,000
Cost of land		30,000
Cost of warehouse		100,000
Rehabilitation Cost		250,000
First year amortization	$250,000 × 1/5	50,000
Reduction in taxes due to		
amortization—1st year	50,000 × 66%	33,000
Sales Price		500,000
Reduction in taxes due to		
amortization over 4 year		
period		132,000

FIGURE 15-1

already *individually* listed in the National Register, Part 1 of the form need not be filled out; it is automatically a certified historic property. Your State Historic Preservation Officer can tell you whether it is individually listed. Part 2 is to get the proposed or completed rehabilitation work certified. Good photographs are critical. Wherever possible, Part 2 should be completed *prior to* starting rehabilitation work. The rehab work is judged on whether it is consistent with the Secretary of the Interior's "Standards for Rehabilitation," a copy of which ten standards can also be secured from your State Historic Preservation Office.

A GOVERNMENT GUIDE ON HOW TO MAKE SURE
A HISTORIC REHAB WILL BE CERTIFIED

A guideline designed by the government to help owners rehabilitate buildings consistent with these "Standards for Rehabilitation" applies to all types of buildings, interiors and exteriors and new and attached construction, and is available from your State Historic Preservation Office and from the U.S. Department of the Interior, Washington D.C. A complete list of State Historic Preservation Officers and their addresses, prepared by the U.S. Department of the Interior, Office of Archeology and Historic Preservation, is presented in Figure 15-2.

HOW TO PROFIT FROM REHABBBING

To make money in real estate and keep most of it through tax depreciation and tax credits, you have to first find these profitable deals. Information, contacts and local knowledge are the paths to real estate wealth.

For example, one such opportunity is found in the many turnaround neighborhoods throughout our land now. Federal and state legislation encourages historic preservation through favorable tax and other incentives. Changing population trends with big bulges of single and childless couples and smaller families make for less bedroom demand, less school demand and *an increasing demand for city living.* There is a growing market, particularly among young people ages 25 to 35, for rehabilitated properties in formerly run-down neighborhoods. To spot these turnaround areas, you have to understand and keep up with these population changes and housing-service demands. You have to know the local situation on a block-

State Historic Preservation Officers

Alabama: Director, Alabama Department of Archives and History, Chairman, Alabama Historical Commission, Archives and History Building, Montgomery, Alabama 36104 **Alaska:** Chief of History and Archeology, Division of Parks, Department of Natural Resources, 619 Warehouse Avenue, Suite 210, Anchorage, Alaska 99501 **American Samoa:** Territorial Historic Preservation Officer, Department of Public Works, Government of American Samoa, Pago Pago, American Samoa 96799 **Arizona:** Chief, Natural and Cultural Resource Conservation Section, Arizona State Parks, 1688 West Adams, Phoenix, Arizona 85007 **Arkansas:** Director, Arkansas Historic Preservation Program, Suite 500, Continental Building, Markham and Main Streets, Little Rock, Arkansas 72201 **California:** Office of Historic Preservation, California Department of Parks & Recreation, P.O. Box 2390, Sacramento, California 95811 **Colorado:** Chairman, State Historical Society, Colorado State Museum, 200 14th Avenue, Denver, Colorado 80203 **Connecticut:** Director, Connecticut Historical Commission, 59 South Prospect Street, Hartford, Connecticut 06106 **Delaware:** Director, Division of Historical and Cultural Affairs, Hall of Records, Dover, Delaware 19901 **District of Columbia:** Director, Department of Housing and Community Development, 1325 G Street, NW., Washington, D.C. 20005 **Florida:** Director, Division of Archives, History and Records Management, Department of State, 401 East Gaines Street, Tallahassee, Florida 32304 **Georgia:** Chief, Historic Preservation Section, Department of Natural Resources, 270 Washington Street, SW., Room 703-C, Atlanta, Georgia 30334 **Guam:** Director of Parks and Recreation, Government of Guam, P.O. Box 682, Agana, Guam 96910 **Hawaii:** Department of Land and Natural Resources, P.O. Box 621, Honolulu, Hawaii 96809 **Idaho:** Historic Preservation Coordinator, Idaho Historical Society, 610 North Julia Davis Drive, Boise, Idaho 83706 **Illinois:** Director, Department of Conservation, 602 State Office Building, 400 South Spring Street, Springfield, Illinois 62706 **Indiana:** Director, Department of Natural Resources, 608 State Office Building, Indianapolis, Indiana 46204 **Iowa:** Director, Iowa State Historical Dept., Division of Historic Preservation, 26 East Market Street, Iowa City, Iowa 52240 **Kansas:** Executive Director, Kansas State Historical Society, 120 West 10th Street, Topeka, Kansas 66612 **Kentucky:** Director, Kentucky Heritage Commission, 104 Bridge Street, Frankfort, Kentucky 40601 **Louisiana:** Secretary, Department of Culture, Recreation, and Tourism, P.O. Box 44361, Baton Rouge, Louisiana 70804 **Maine:** Director, Maine Historic Preservation Commission, 31 Western Avenue, Augusta, Maine 04330 **Maryland:** John Shaw House, 21 State Circle, Annapolis, Maryland 21401 **Massachusetts:** Executive Director, Massachusetts Historical Commission, 294 Washington Street, Boston, Massachusetts 02108 **Michigan:** Director, Michigan History Division, Department of State, Lansing, Michigan 48918 **Minnesota:** Director, Minnesota Historical Society, 690 Cedar Street, St. Paul, Minnesota 55101 **Mississippi:** Director, State of Mississippi, Department of Archives and History, P.O. Box 571, Jackson, Mississippi 39205 **Missouri:** Director, State Department of Natural Resources, 1014 Madison Street, Jefferson City, Missouri 65101 **Montana:** Director, Montana Historical Society, 225 North Roberts Street, Veterans' Memorial Building, Helena, Montana 59601 **Nebraska:** 10

Director, The Nebraska State Historical Society, 1500 R Street, Lincoln, Nebraska 68508 **Nevada:** Division of Historic Preservation and Archeology, Department of Conservation & Natural Resources, Nye Building, 201 South Fall Street, Carson City, Nevada 89710 **New Hampshire:** Commissioner, Department of Resources, and Economic Development, P.O. Box 846, Concord, New Hampshire 03301 **New Jersey:** Commissioner, Department of Environmental Protection, P.O. Box 1420, Trenton, New Jersey 08625 **New Mexico:** State Planning Office, 505 Don Gaspar, Santa Fe, New Mexico 87503 **New York:** Commissioner, Parks and Recreation, Agency Building #1, Empire State Plaza, Albany, New York 12238 **North Carolina:** Director, Division of Archives and History, Department of Cultural Resources, 109 East Jones Street, Raleigh, North Carolina 27611 **North Dakota:** Superintendent, State Historical Society of North Dakota, Liberty Memorial Building, Bismarck, North Dakota 58501 **Oklahoma:** 235 Pasteur Building, 1111 North Lee, Oklahoma City, Oklahoma 73103 **Oregon:** State Parks Superintendent, 525 Trade Street, SE., Salem, Oregon 97310 **Pennsylvania:** Executive Director, Pennsylvania Historical and Museum Commission, P.O. Box 1026, Harrisburg, Pennsylvania 17120 **Commonwealth of Puerto Rico:** Institute of Puerto Rico Culture, Apartado 4184, San Juan, Puerto Rico 00905 **Rhode Island:** Director, Rhode Island Department of Community Affairs, 150 Washington Street, Providence, Rhode Island 02903 **South Carolina:** Director, State Archives Department, 1430 Senate Street, Columbia, South Carolina 29211 **South Dakota:** Historical Preservation Center, University of South Dakota, Alumni House, Vermillion, South Dakota 57069 **Tennessee:** Executive Director, Tennessee Historical Commission, 170 Second Avenue North, Suite 100, Nashville, Tennessee 37219 **Texas:** Executive Director, Texas State Historical Commission, P.O. Box 12276, Capitol Station, Austin, Texas 78711 **Trust Territory of The Pacific Islands:** Land Resources Branch, Department of Resources & Development, Trust Territory of the Pacific Islands, Saipan, Mariana Islands 96950 **Utah:** Executive Director, Department of Development Services, Room 104, State Capitol, Salt Lake City, Utah 84114 **Vermont:** Director, Vermont Division for Historic Preservation, Pavilion Office Building, Montpelier, Vermont 05602 **Virginia:** Virginia Historic Landmarks Commission, 221 Governor Street, Richmond, Virginia 23219 **Virgin Islands:** Planning Director, Virgin Islands Planning Board, Charlotte Amalie, St. Thomas, Virgin Islands 00801 **Washington:** State Office of Archeology & Historic Preservation, 7150 Cleanwater Lane, Olympia, Washington 98504 **West Virginia:** Historic Preservation Unit, Department of Culture and History, State Capitol Complex, Charleston, West Virginia 25305 **Wisconsin:** Director, State Historical Society of Wisconsin, 816 State Street, Madison, Wisconsin 53706 **Wyoming:** Director, Wyoming Recreation Commission, 604 East 25th Street, Box 309, Cheyenne, Wyoming 82001 **National Trust for Historic Preservation:** President, National Trust for Historic Preservation, 740 Jackson Place, NW., Washington, D.C. 20006

THIS LEAFLET WAS PREPARED BY
THE OFFICE OF ARCHEOLOGY AND
HISTORIC PRESERVATION

HERITAGE CONSERVATION AND
RECREATION SERVICE
U.S. DEPARTMENT OF THE INTERIOR
WASHINGTON, D.C.

☆ GPO : 1978 O – 271-542

FIGURE 15-2

by-block basis. Revitalization of neighborhoods feeds upon prior rehabilitation. Young people, many of them affluent professional people, spread the word as to the "in" neighborhoods. Real estate as ever is dynamic. The old decaying block of yesterday can become the beautiful restored block of brownstones tomorrow.

Fifteen years ago, I appraised dilapidated row houses in old sections of Brooklyn for $12,000 each. The same houses sell today for $90,000 up for the shell, $200,000 up if restored.

Excellent location sources are government agencies which have lists of properties for sale, some of them in such potential turnaround areas. The FHA (HUD) and VA regularly publish lists of their foreclosed, for-sale properties. These lists are yours for the asking from the local offices of these agencies which even provide very good financing with low downpayments to buyers.

Rehabbing techniques in turnaround areas fall into three parts:

- *First*, as always, is location. You have to spot the block or neighborhood that will appeal to this new market of affluent sophisticated young singles and couples.
- *Second*, you have to check out the property. The building must be sound and able to accommodate an overhaul.
- *Third*, the price must be right and financing must be available.

RECYCLING HISTORIC RAILROAD STATIONS— A UNIQUE, LITTLE-KNOWN PROFIT OPPORTUNITY

The imaginative reuse of historic railroad stations is a phenomenon beginning to occur across the country. There is a very good supply—more than 20,000 railroad stations, some neglected and decaying but practically all centrally well located in most localities.

These abandoned stations usually offer a rich variety of architectural style and detail. Energy efficient and structurally sound, these many thousands of remaining stations offer vast potential for exciting and imaginative rehabilitation, reuse and profit. Even semi-used stations which are still on active rail passenger routes such as the Northeast, Chicago-Detroit and Los Angles-San Diego corridors are available for compatible, rehabilitated, multi-use such as restaurants, shops and other commercial operations.

You are in the best local position to get in on this recycling of historic railroad stations. You can get special help and guidance from the U.S. Department of Transportation, Office of Environment and

Safety, Washington, D.C. 20590, including basic guidelines for successful projects and feasibility procedures. A manual on "Recycling Historic Stations" is also available from the Superintendent of Documents, Washington, D.C.

In addition to private funding by local lenders, grants and loans are available under certain conditions for such railroad renovations from the following government sources in their Washington and regional offices:

> General Services Administration (GSA)
> Economic Development Administration (EDA)
> Regional Development Commissions (Dept. of Commerce)
> Small Business Administration (SBA)
> Farmers Home Administration (Dept. of Agriculture)

The National Trust for Historic Preservation, 740 Jackson Place, N.W., Washington, DC. 20006, a private non-profit organization, also offers grants and loans under certain conditions to members.

Two Case Histories of Successful Station Renovations

The case histories illustrated in Figures 15-3 and 15-4 show how two local railroad stations were recycled successfully into commercial and multi-uses.

HISTORICAL PROPERTIES: A SUMMARY OF THEIR LITTLE-KNOWN PROFIT POSSIBILITIES

This chapter has been entirely devoted to that little-known modern technique of rehabilitating historic properties. You can reap large benefits in your own local area from such renovations:

1. *Income tax savings.*
2. *Rental income.*
3. *Personal use* and occupany, if desired, of part or all of such restored, architecturally appealing residential or commercial space.
4. *Resale and profit* of such renovated historical properties which have had income flow restored.

If you follow the guidelines developed here, there is a great market for restored properties. You can sell them through normal real estate channels like real estate brokers or through advertising. Or you can hold and lease for maximum tax benefit.

The Depot Drive-Up Bank in former Rock Island Depot.

This early recycling effort illustrates the favorable public image station reuse can have and the importance of choosing a use which is compatible with the building and marketable in the given location.

Location:	Lincoln, Nebraska, population 180,000, in commercial area on fringe of CBD
Owner:	Citibank & Trust Company, 14th and M, Lincoln, Nebraska 68501
Present Use:	Drive-in branch bank, two commercial spaces
Building Date, Style:	1893, Chateauesque style
Original Architect:	P. Day, Chief Engineer, Chicago, Rock Island and Pacific Railroad
Reuse Architect:	Clark and Enersen/Olsson, Burroughs and Thomsen, Lincoln, Nebraska
Project Cost:	$300,000; including special banking equipment
Acquisition Cost:	$75,000; another $55,000 to settle suit brought by abutters
Gross Floor Area:	3,750 square feet
Financing:	Private, conventional mortgage
Federal Funds:	None
State Funds:	None
Renovation Started:	April, 1968
Renovation Completed:	June, 1969
Handicapped Accessibility:	Drive-in banking island provides full access from automobiles.

CHICAGO, ROCK ISLAND AND PACIFIC DEPOT

LINCOLN, NEBRASKA

FIGURE 15-3

Union Station combines a restaurant and offices with a busy Amtrak station.

An architect-developer entity, a sound scheme to leverage public and private monies, and the relentless devotion of local preservationists were essential to the successful multi-use of this station.

UNION STATION NEW LONDON, CONNECTICUT

Location:	New London, Connecticut, population 31,650, urban downtown location
Owner:	Union Station Associates of New London, 77 N. Washington Street, Boston, Massachusetts 02114
Present Use:	Train station, restaurant, offices
Project Cost:	$835,236
Building Date, Style:	1886, Romanesque Revival
Original Architect:	Henry Hobson Richardson
Reuse Architect:	Anderson Notter Finegold Inc., Boston, Massachusetts
Acquisition Cost:	$11,400
Gross Floor Area:	22,000 square feet
Net Floor Area:	17,680 square feet
Financing:	Private, conventional mortgage with Federal grants and loans
Federal Funds:	HUD Community Development Block Grant; two National Register grants; National Trust grant and loan
State Funds:	None
Renovation Started:	October, 1975
Renovation Completed:	August 1978
Handicapped Accessibility:	Full accessibility for the handicapped to all floors except restaurant mezzanine by ramp and elevator.

FIGURE 15-4

16

How to Cash In on Condominiums and Cooperatives

This chapter shows you how to profit from the real estate wave of the future—condominiums and cooperatives. The first section sets forth examples and details of this ancient legal condominium tool which has been adapted to modern real estate. A companion section specifies exactly the differences between condominiums and cooperatives. You are shown how important your lawyer's work is to these new, very legal ways of developing and profiting from cooperatives and condominiums. Finally, there is a condominium/cooperative glossary.

CONDOMINIUM, AN ANCIENT TOOL FOR MODERN PROFITS

For most of its history, America was one of the few developed countries that did not use condominiums in real estate. Most other modern, urbanized countries have been buying and selling condominiums down through the centuries since ancient Babylon started this type of real estate ownership.

We Americans, however, don't do things by halves. We may not have understood or had condominium enabling laws for about 2500 years. However, we're sure making up for the delay quickly now. The last ten years have seen condominiums accepted everywhere by differing state enabling laws. There is even a federal nationally recommended model condominium law which probably will be enacted soon by most states. In the last few years, 50,000 apartments in Chicago have been converted to condominiums. There are new condominium complexes and apartment conversions going on in Boston, Denver, Atlanta, Los Angeles, Miami, San Francisco, Seattle and Washington, D.C. All types of other residences besides apartments are going condominium. Industrial, commercial and office buildings are even joining this surge to condominiums. Economists predict that by the year 2000, *most new homes* will be purchased under some form of condominium ownership! You don't have to become a big developer to get in on these condo profits. You just have to learn the new condo ways shown here and apply your local knowledge.

Examples of Condo Profits

Condos are not only feasible now but also very, very profitable. One small builder in southeastern New York discovered condominiums recently. He used this knowledge to market his semi-attached two-family houses. Now instead of selling these two two-family houses which are built on *one* building plot to one buyer for $150,000, he sells each two-family house as a condominium for $90,000. It cost him an additional $500 in legal costs for each of his two-family units to restructure them legally as condominiums, but physically they remained the same. The only difference was that he made almost $30,000 more from each pair of two-family dwelling improvements on each plot.

Recently, in only three years, Florida went from an overhang of unsold condominiums to a boom. You find them in every price range, everywhere. From $30,000 condos in Florida to $300,000 condos in Hawaii, people wait in line when sales open on new projects to buy them for dwelling or resale profit purposes.

One New Jersey project during the same recent three-year period went from half-empty units for sale at $60,000 to a list waiting to buy any of the same units as they became available—at $125,000!

Acceptance is universal now. Profits are skyrocketing because this pent-up demand is being force-fed by inflation and by post-WWII baby-boom people now mainly in their late twenties who have apparently accepted this modern way of life.

How do you get into this condo profit wave of the future? Do you have to buy or build a skyscraper luxury apartment building as so many big condo builders and converters are doing today? Do you need millions to develop large tracts with hundreds of condo units? These are all excellent profit examples of where the pros are putting their money today. If you have money to invest, by all means consider condominiums. You'll like the profits.

However, the beauty of condominiums is that they cover the whole gamut of real estate, from the very large to the very small. Let me suggest the many large and small ways you can cash in on this condominium boom now and into your future:

SUCCESSFUL WAYS TO
GET IN ON THE CONDO BOOM

• *Buy existing two-family houses.* This is a particularly imaginative use of the condominium tool. You can put your local knowledge to work here for great profits. Most two-families are in multiple zones. So, you buy the two-family building, spend about $1000 for legal condominium work, then sell *each half* of the building separately. Condominium here is a case of adding one plus one and getting three. For example, say you buy a two-family building in your area for $60,000. You spend that $1000 extra for the legal condominium documents. Then you sell *each unit* for $45,000. So, 1 + 1 = 3—or how to make a $29,000 profit.

• *Buy condominium units.* If you don't want to buy and convert or build, all you have to do is buy existing already built or converted units and watch your investment race ahead of inflation. Not only that but also you can live in it while you wait to sell it. Some investors buy one or more units and then rent them while they wait for capital appreciation and resale profits.

• *Buy and convert apartment buildings.* Whether a few or many apartment units are involved, tax laws make it more profitable for a seller to sell his rental apartment building to one buyer rather than do the condo conversion himself. A long-term owner selling his building is taxed at capital gain rates. If he converted the building himself, he would be taxed at the much higher ordinary income rate, up to 70%. The condominium converter he sells the whole building to instead, can get profits as high as 30% over what was paid to buy the building, spruce up the units and pay for the legal work to set up the condominium papers. Remember, you are selling the units one by one on a retail basis if you do the condominium converting. You bought it at a wholesale price. And you're selling into a big demand from modern sophisticated buyers who want to own their homes for their own tax deductions and their own profits when they sell.

• *Build or convert commercial, industrial and office buildings.* This non-residential condominium trend is just starting and is gain-ing acceptance and profits in professional, medical office buildings and small neighborhood shopping centers particularly.

• *Build condo townhouse developments.* Small parcels in the suburbs and in the cities can now be developed on a condominium basis. Lengthy subdivision processing is cut down and common areas like parking, lawns, exterior maintenance make for better layout, function, sales and profits.

CONDOS CAN BE ALMOST ANYTHING

What is a condominium? Condominium simply means individual ownership of one's own unit in a multi-unit project. It can be in a high-rise building (over six stories), a low-rise building, an attached townhouse, a two-family building, a four-plex, even a detached single-unit dwelling. High-rise and low-rise condos have individual ownerships above and below individual units while horizontal units like condo townhouse do not. In *all* types of condominiums, the land below the structure is owned in common estate by all owners as one part of the common elements.

CONDO DIFFERENCES ANALYZED

The basic difference that distinguishes condominiums from fee simple ownership is the deed. A conventional property deed on an improved property owned in fee simple describes the plot in two dimensions, length and width, all around its boundaries, and includes all improvements within these described boundaries. A condominium master deed also describes the land in two dimensions but then goes into three dimensions to describe the building(s) and the individual units including depth and height. The owner of each individual unit in a condominium multi-unit building gets only a short deed of ownership, identifying his unit by a designated number and referring to the master deed, which is recorded and filed legally with local authority the same as any other real estate deed. The master deed also describes the common elements of the condominium estate which all unit owners share in ownership and in maintenance charges, including streets, utilities, recreational facilities, parking, lights, grounds, building structure (on the outside of each unit's interior paint film and floor finish, generally), building foundations, basements and roofs.

Perhaps that's why it took almost 2500 years for condominiums to get accepted here. New terms, complicated legal start-up process-ing and a need for condominium unit owners to cooperate with each other for their mutual economic good are all-important factors in condominiums. The economic pressure of our denser modern society and the high cost of land and construction are what have finally made condominiums feasible.

Even though slightly more complicated, this is where much of the real estate action is now and will be in the foreseeable future. To make profits, you have to join in this action. However, as in all real estate investment, you have to know what you're doing *before* you sign that deposit check and become committed. In condominiums, this is particularly important, because it is a comparatively new field and it's initially and legally more complex. Here are special condo step-by-step procedures to make sure that you don't get carried away by the condo boom and wind up with a sour lemon investment. A half-sold condominium with half-built improvements can leave the buyers real problems if the condo builder fails to complete the com-plex. Condo profits await informed, objective buyers. If you're buying one condo unit or the whole building, you still have to do it the right way to ensure profits.

KEY STEPS FOR CONDO PROFITS

Step 1. Inspect site and location. Inspect and review for location, access to transportation and roads, construction, light, air view. Is the plan functional for access by car and by pedestrian paths? Recreational facilities commensurate with project size? On existing projects, check to see if there is a high tenant occupany which may mean a poor sales market.

Step 2. Analyze master deed and bylaws. On existing projects, review the master deed and bylaws; on proposed projects, study the prospectus for number of units and project information on rights, con-ditions and limitations. Check particularly to see if the developer has locked the buyers into long-term self-serving covenants or mainte-nance contracts and to make sure there are no major restrictions against resale by individual condo owners.

Step 3. Compare condo to competitive projects. Shop around. Re-search the market for demand, sales activity, price ranges. Remember, there's a boom on condominiums, but don't be in a rush to pay tomor-row's prices today. They may represent your profits of tomorrow. Hire a professional appraiser if in doubt as to current value.

Step 4. Check to make sure that everything promised is in. If a large complex is involved, are promised amenities like tennis courts in and paid for? Are roads, utilities in?

Step 5. Check to see that ownership interests are fair. In condominiums, if all units are equal and sold for same price, then each unit has an equal interest in common facilities and in maintenance obligations. Or if various types are involved, then size of units or selling price can be used to proportion ownership fairly.

Step 6. Check as to whether or not parking is adequate. Look for minimum 1½ parking spaces times the number of units plus guest parking.

Step 7. Analyze budget. This should include adequacy of reserves for maintenance and replacement of common elements.

Step 8. Analyze assessment. Review the monthly maintenance charge. (On proposed projects, it's usually underestimated.)

Step 9. Inspect for repairs. Check unit for required repairs if existing. Check complex for condition of roads, building exteriors, common elements.

Step 10. Use an attorney experienced in condominiums. He can help in much of this review and to close the sale.

PROCEDURE FOR THE CONDO CONVERTER

Step 1. Hire a condominium attorney. For the condo converter this step comes first. You need his advice on the condo laws in your area before you even start looking for the property.

Step 2. Search for the property. Whether for a two-family dwelling or a 100± unit apartment house or a non-residential property, condo conversion technique is the same. You can use the same feasibility-location-building inspection checklists in Chapter 12. Condominium conversion doesn't change the physical nature of buildings and land, except in cases where renovation or alteration is involved. Condo restructuring itself is a strictly legal change which alters the property from a single ownership, multiple tenancy to a multiple ownership of the individual units. Each apartment gets an individual owner.

Step 3. Hire professionals. If the building needs major overhaul to make it salable as individual units or if more units can be made, hire an architect. If all that is needed is a condo "paper" conversion, then hire a professional appraiser to give you a current valuation report.

Step 4. Buy the building. If it can meet local condo laws and the appraisal warrants, buy the building.

Step 5. Attorney draws the documents. Your attorney draws up the condominium documents, the bylaws, the prospectus, and files the papers with the governing state and and/or municipal authorities.

Step 6. Sell the units. Once the papers are approved, you can start selling the units to tenants and investors in accordance with the laws in your community. (There are special rights for existing tenants in practically all condominium laws.)

HOW TO TELL A CONDO FROM A CO-OP

Condominium-Cooperative Differences

In some localities, such as New York City, cooperatives or "co-ops" are the rule rather than condominiums because special laws make co-ops more feasible and quicker to consummate than condominiums.

In many ways, co-ops are similar to condominiums. In the most important way, there is also a runaway inflation in housing prices of co-ops as in condominiums. For example, during one *nine-month* period recently, the average selling prices of converted co-op apartments in New York City went from $16,500 to $25,000 *per room.* People are flocking back, particularly to Manhattan for its urban amenities. It is estimated that rentals for good city apartments will soon be up to $1000 a room. So the same pressures that make for condominium conversion elsewhere create cooperatives in New York City. The cooperative means cooperative or joint operation of a housing development by those who live in it. In a cooperative, the co-op corporation owns all the property including the individual units. A member of a cooperative does not directly own his dwelling unit. He owns a membership stock certificate in the cooperative corporation as a board member or voter. The corporation not only holds title to the whole property but it also pays the mortgage payments, taxes and other obligations to finance and operate the development. Each member pays his proportionate share of the annual budget. Each member is entitled to his proportionate share of the real estate taxes and mortgage interest paid by the corporation for his personal income tax. If a member wants to leave the cooperative, he sells his membership certificate (not his unit) in accordance with value and rules set forth in the cooperative corporation bylaws.

The basic difference between a cooperative and a condominium is that a cooperative corporation owns everything and a condominium association owns nothing. A condominium owner owns his individual estate (or unit) and an individual interest in the common estate (or common elements). An owner of an individual condo unit pays his own mortgage and taxes as well as his monthly assessment for common element costs. The condo owner can sell or lease his unit directly, sometimes having to give first refusal to purchase for a limited time to the Condominium Council representing the other owners.

It is important to know these differences because the laws in a number of places like New York City still favor cooperatives over condominiums. Your approach for cooperative profits is basically the same as in the condo procedure. There are the specific technical differences like the cooperative stock corporation which must be formed to take the ownership of the property which the unit owners share. There are the additional restrictions in co-ops against the free individual exercise of ownership rights to buy and sell. Co-ops have been around much longer here than condos, yet condos appear to be the real estate wave of the future. However, you can still use and profit from cooperative real estate investments wherever these forms of real estate ownership are more favorable. You go where the real estate action is.

YOUR CONDOMINIUM ATTORNEY

Your condo lawyer is the key man. The condo boom is here. Condo profits are there in the future. Working it out is more complicated than conventional real estate profit making. The one who can tie all this together is the lawyer knowledgeable and experienced in condominiums.

It costs more in fees to have him review and advise on existing condo documents or to draw up master deeds and bylaws on proposed new or converted condos. The profits are worth the extra fees. Just for example, the experienced condo lawyer works with your surveyor and/or architect on a new or converted condo to write the basic master deed for the entire property in a whole new and different way than in the normal deed description. He doesn't just describe the land by its surface boundary dimensions. He takes off into space (and delves subsurface into basement areas) to describe the property by depth and height as well. This "air space" or volume-type of deed description can best be visualized by considering, say, a two-bedroom living unit in a low-rise six-story condominium. He would start this unit's deed description at one corner of the entry foyer floor, describe the distances and directions around the floor of the entire living unit (beneath the film of wall paint and floor finish), come back to the same beginning point of the entry foyer corner, but then go up that corner to the ceiling, go all around the ceilings back to the same beginning point to encompass and describe the legal ownership of that two-bedroom condominium unit.

This master deed is only one illustration of what the competent attorney does for you in real estate condominiums. He also is there to keep you out of trouble in these complex yet very profitable real estate condominiums.

A CONDOMINIUM/COOPERATIVE DICTIONARY

The HUD Glossary (HUD-365-H(4)) of special condominium and cooperative terms presented here will help you understand and cash in on these very special real estate profit opportunities.

GLOSSARY

ABSTRACT—A summary of the history of the legal title to a piece of property.

AMORTIZATION—Provision for gradually paying off the principal amount of a loan, such as a mortgage loan, at the time of each payment of interest. For example, as each payment toward principal is made, the mortgage amount is reduced or amortized by that amount.

APPRAISAL—An evaluation of the property to determine its value. An appraisal is concerned chiefly with market value—what the unit would sell for in the market place.

ASSESSMENT (Operating)—Proportionate share of the budgeted annual cost to maintain physically the common areas and elements of a condominium and to maintain sufficient reserves to assure financial stability. The annual assessment is reduced to monthly charges payable to the Association of owners.

ASSESSMENT (Special)—An assessment for some special purpose or because of inadequate budgeting of operating expenses.

CAVEAT—A warning or notice to take heed such as a clause in a document which is meant to be a warning.

CERTIFICATE OF TITLE—Like a car title, this is the paper that signifies ownership of a unit. It usually contains a legal description of the unit and its relationship to the condominium.

CLOSING COSTS—Cost in addition to the price of a unit and its undivided interest in the common estate including mortgage service charge, title search, insurance and transfer of ownership charges paid each time the unit is resold or refinanced.

CLOSING DAY—The date on which the title for property passes from the seller to the buyer and/or the date on which the borrower signs the mortgage.

COMMON AREA OR COMMON ESTATE—Generally, this encompasses all of a condominium which is not specifically delineated and described as dwelling or commercial units.

COMMON OR UNDIVIDED INTEREST—Joint ownership with other fee owners of all land and areas within the structures that are not described as individually owned units. The interest is defined by a percentage of a total area but not actually divided into individual parts.

CONDOMINIUM ASSOCIATION, ASSOCIATION OF OWNERS, CONDOMINIUM ASSOCIATION BOARD OF DIRECTORS, OR COUNCIL OF CO-OWNERS—The governing body of a condominium, elected by and from among the owners upon conveyance of titles to the individual owners by the Grantor. Its authority to operate comes from the Declaration. It must operate within the framework of the Bylaws.

CONDOMINIUM REGIME—The mode of self-rule established when condominium documents are recorded. The term also refers to all the documents necessary to legally constitute a condominium and to permit it to operate as such.

CONVEY—To transfer title from one person to another.

COVENANT—A promise usually in the form of a recorded agreement when used as a part of the language of real estate.

COOPERATIVE HOUSING—A housing corporation or a group of dwellings owned by residents and operated for the benefit of resident members of the corporation by their elected Board of Directors. The resident occupies but does not own his unit. Rather, he owns a share of stock or membership certificate in the total enterprise.

DECLARATION—A document which contains conditions, covenants and restrictions governing the sale, ownership, use and disposition of property within the framework of applicable State condominium laws.

DEED—A document used to transfer a fee simple interest in the unit together with an undivided interest in the common estate in the case of condominium title transfers.

DELINEATE—To describe the physical boundaries of a dwelling unit in a condominium.

DEPRECIATION—A decline in the value of a dwelling unit as the result of wear and tear, adverse changes in the neighborhood and its patterns, or for any other reason.

EARNEST MONEY OR SUBSCRIPTION MONEY—The deposit money given to the seller by the potential buyer to show that he is serious about buying the dwelling. If the deal goes through, the earnest money is applied against the downpayment. If the deal does not go through, through no fault of the seller, it may be forfeited.

EASEMENT RIGHTS—A right of way granted to a person or company authorizing access to or over the owner's land. Water, sewer, and electric companies often have easement rights across private property.

EASEMENT—A right or privilege a person or group of people may have in property owned by one or more other persons.

ENCUMBRANCE—A claim or lien attached to real property, such as a mortgage or unsatisfied debt incurred with respect to the property.

EQUITY—Increase in value of ownership interest in the unit as the owner reduces his debt by paying off his mortgage, and from market value appreciation.

ESCROW FUNDS—Subscription or downpayments required to be held unused, until the condominium regime is recorded on the property and titles are conveyed to each buyer. Escrows are usually used in each resale situation. The deed is held in escrow until all conditions of the sale (including any prepayments) have been met. Other escrow accounts are used to accumulate monthly tax and insurance payments until the taxes and insurance are actually due.

GRANTOR—The owner of the property which is being subdivided into a multiple number of individual unit estates under a condominium regime.

LATENT DEFECT BOND—One type is an assurance required by HUD-FHA that defects due to faulty materials and workmanship, which are found within a year of the date of completion, will be corrected.

LEASEHOLD INTEREST—The right to use a property under certain conditions which does not carry with it the rights of ownership.

LIABILITY AND HAZARD INSURANCE—Insurance to protect against negligent actions of the Association of owners and damages caused to property by fire, windstorm and other common hazards.

LIEN—A claim recorded against a property as security for payment of a just debt.

MORTGAGE COMMITMENT—The written notice from the bank or other lender saying that it will advance the mortgage funds in a specified amount to enable one to buy the unit.

MORTAGE DISCOUNT "POINTS"—Discounts (points) are a one-time charge assessed by a lending institution to increase the yield from the mortgage loan to a competitive position with the yield from other types of investments.

MORTGAGEE—The bank or lender who loans the money to the mortgagor.

MORTGAGE INSURANCE PREMIUM—The payment made by a borrower to the lender for transmittal to HUD-FHA to help defray the cost of the FHA mortgage insurance program and provide a reserve fund to protect lenders against loss in insured mortgage transactions. In the case of an FHA insured mortgage this represents an annual rate of one-half of one percent paid by the mortgagor on a monthly basis to FHA. Non-government mortgage insurance companies have a similar premium.

MORTGAGE LOAN (INDIVIDUAL UNITS)—The amount loaned by the lender (mortgagee) to the individual owner (mortgagor) necessary to purchase the unit.

MORTGAGE LOAN (PROJECT)—Provides money to the builder/developer to acquire the land and construct the condominium. This loan should be paid off in full by the cash and individual mortgage loans that come into existence when all sales have been consummated. At such time the condominium individual units must be free and clear of all liens and all individual unit mortgages must be first mortgages assumed by owners of the units.

MORTGAGE LOAN (HUD-FHA INSURED)—The lender is insured by HUD-FHA against default by the mortgagor to induce the lender to lend a larger sum to the purchaser. The loan limits are established by HUD-FHA.

MORTGAGOR—The homeowner who applies for, receives and is obligated to repay a mortgage loan on a property he has purchased.

PLAT AND PLANS—Drawings used by surveyors and architects to show the exact location of utilities, streets, buildings and units within the buildings, in relation to the boundary lines of the total property. They may also show units, common areas and restricted areas.

PREPAID EXPENSES—The initial deposit at time of closing, for taxes and the subsequent monthly deposits made to the lender for that purpose. Hazard insurance is not a mortgage payment under the individual unit mortgage.

REPAIR AND MAINTENANCE—The costs incurred in replacing damaged items or maintaining housing systems to prevent damage. In a condominium the owner is responsible for repairing and maintaining the dwelling unit and the condominium Association is responsible for repairing and maintaining the common areas. The owner only pays his proportionate share of the cost to the Association.

RESERVE FUNDS (REPLACEMENT)—Funds which are set aside in escrow from monthly payments to replace common elements, such as roofs, at some future date.

RESERVE FUNDS (GENERAL OPERATING)—Funds which are accumulated on a monthly basis to provide a cushion of capital to be used when and if a contingency arises.

STATUTE—A law passed by a legislative body and set forth in a formal document, for example the Horizontal Property Act of Puerto Rico.

TAXES—Local real estate assessments which are levied on the individual units and not on the condominium Association.

TITLE—The evidence of a person's legal right to possession of property, normally in the form of a deed.

TITLE COMPANY—A company that specializes in insuring title to property.

TITLE INSURANCE—Special insurance which usually protects lenders against loss of their interest in property due to unforeseen occurrences that might be traced to legal flaws in previous ownerships. An owner can protect his interest by purchasing separate coverage. A mortgagee's policy, as distinguished from an owner's policy, usually protects only the lender in an amount equal to the outstanding balance of the mortgage loan.

TITLE SEARCH OR EXAMINATION—A check of the title records, generally at the local courthouse, to make sure you are buying the dwelling from the legal owner and that there are no liens, overdue special assessments, other claims, outstanding restrictive covenants or other defects in title filed in the record.

UNDIVIDED INTEREST—In condominium law, the joint ownership of common areas in which the individual percentages are known but are not applied to separate the areas physically. This situation is similar to the joint ownership of an automobile or home by husband and wife.

UNIT VALUE RATIO—A percentage developed by dividing the appraised value of a unit by the total value of all units. The percentage attaches to the dwelling unit and determines the percentage of value of the common estate attached to that unit, the percentage of votes the owner of the unit has in the government of the common estate, and the percentage of operating costs of the common areas the respective unit owner must bear.

Index